FAITH IN ACTION

FAITH IN ACTION

A Guide for Activists, Advocates, and Allies

FORTRESS PRESS

MINNEAPOLIS

Cover design: Brad Norr
Book design: Rob Dewey and Ivy Palmer Skrade

Print ISBN: 978-1-5064-3256-4
eBook ISBN: 978-1-5064-4335-5

The paper used in this publication meets the minimum requirements
of American National Standard for Information Sciences — Permanence
of Paper for Printed Library Materials, ANSI Z329.48-1984.

Manufactured in the U.S.A.

CONTENTS

Guides

CONTRIBUTORS

Marques Armstrong is cofounder of Black Pearl LLC, a multifaceted consulting firm focused on racial equity. He is also CEO and founder of Hope & Healing Counseling Services and a trained community organizer and public-policy advocate.

Sharon Betcher is an independent scholar and writer, specializing in the area of disability theology. She is the author of *Spirit and the Politics of Disablement* (Fortress Press, 2007) and *Spirit and the Obligation of Social Flesh* (2013).

Bethany Bradley was a cofounder of the Women's March on Washington: MN March and continues to serve as a member of the Steering Committee for the Women's March Minnesota organization. She has a background in nonprofit event planning, branding, and media coordination.

DeWayne Davis is senior pastor at All God's Children Metropolitan Community Church in Minneapolis. He serves on the Public Policy Team of the MCC's Global Justice Institute, representing the denomination's public-policy advocacy initiatives at the federal level. He also recently served as the domestic policy analyst in the Episcopal Church's Office of Government Relations and worked as a congressional aide before his ministry career.

Christopher Zumski Finke is a freelance journalist and reporter for *Yes! Magazine*, covering culture, justice, and citizen engagement. He is editor of *The Stake*, a pop culture and politics website. He worked in public policy for Wind on the Wires, an advocacy group specializing in renewable energy.

Sonja Hagander is university pastor, director of ministries, and associate director of the Christensen Center for Vocation at Augsburg University, the Evangelical Lutheran Church in America's most diverse college.

Jaylani Hussein is executive director of the Minnesota chapter of the Council on American-Islamic Relations (CAIR-MN). In 2013, he created Zeila Consultants to develop and offer cross-cultural training workshops on East African cultures.

Jim Bear Jacobs is a member of the Stockbridge-Munsee Mohican Nation. He is a cultural facilitator in the Twin Cities, working to raise the public's awareness of American Indian causes, and currently serves as an associate pastor at Church of All Nations in Columbia Heights, Minnesota.

Nekima Levy-Pounds is an attorney, scholar, and national expert on issues of race. She was a professor of law at the University of St. Thomas for 13 years and also served as an adviser to Black Lives Matter Minneapolis before starting her own consulting company, Black Pearl LLC. She ran for mayor of Minneapolis in 2017.

Dee McIntosh is pastor of LightHouse MPLS, a Covenant Church plant in Minneapolis. She is a founding member of Black Clergy United for Change, a collective of Black clergy committed to racial justice and social transformation.

Kellie Rock is coordinator of refugee arrival services for Arrive Ministries, a Christian nonprofit organization dedicated to the cause of the refugee and immigrant.

Javen Swanson is associate pastor at Gloria Dei Lutheran Church in St. Paul. He has previously worked as a community organizer with OutFront Minnesota and the Minnesotans United for All Families campaign, and was the interim faith work director for the National LGBTQ Task Force.

INTRODUCTION

On January 21, 2017, millions of people marched in the streets across the United States and around the globe to advocate for fundamental human rights. A week later, thousands more held rallies and protests at airports and in cities to advocate for the rights of refugees and immigrants. Millions of Americans are becoming politically and socially active in a way that they never have before. Those who are just beginning to pay attention to long-standing issues of disparity, oppression, and injustice are joining in with those who have been on the front lines of these issues for decades. Maybe you're one of the people who recently attended a protest or a rally for the first time. Maybe you'd like to be.

You want to make the world a better place. This resource can help.

This book offers primers on a whole range of topics, from racial justice to environmental concerns, from women's equality to disability rights, from mass incarceration to immigration, from LGBTQIA equality to Native Peoples' rights. But none of these topics operate in a vacuum. In fact, you'll notice significant overlap between topics. The wage gap between women and men is made much starker when racial differences are taken into account. The causes of disability are deeply rooted in issues of environmental misuse. We are not singly defined by our gender, or our socioeconomic status, or our race. Each of these elements in our identity makes up part of a greater whole with intersecting implications for our privilege and our disadvantage.

Because of this, we did not attempt to divide the book into chapters, sections, or parts. Well, we did, but we quickly realized how futile the exercise was. Instead, we provide you with short four-page offerings on more than thirty essential topics for would-be activists in today's world. Each topic will include practical suggestions for what you can do to make a difference in your community. But more than a to-do list, this book will broaden and deepen your perspective on these issues and challenge your assumptions. When you step out into the world to be an activist, advocate, and ally, you'll have the tools (and confidence) you'll need to make a real impact.

The contributors to this volume, introduced on page 7, are people of faith. Our values—equity, justice, human dignity, care for the earth—are all rooted in our faith and in the belief that all people are beloved children of God. If you are similarly rooted in faith, you'll recognize those themes and values throughout the book. But there are countless pathways that lead a person to working for justice, and many have nothing to do with faith. All are welcome to this resource, and we hope you'll find it meaningful and valuable, no matter what drew you to it.

Faith is not a prerequisite for working toward justice. But *Faith in Action* believes that the truest expression of faith is one that acts for the good of the world.

WE'RE ALL IMMIGRANTS

You might know . . .

America is a nation
of immigrants.

But maybe you've never thought about . . .

The phrase "we're all immigrants" erases the many
Americans who did not immigrate here—especially
those who are Native Peoples and those who were
brought here against their will as slaves. Many
Americans are comfortable celebrating immigrants
who came to this country decades ago—immigrants
from Ireland, Germany, and Scandinavia, for example.
In fact, we have festivals, national observances, and
commemorative months for many of these immigrant
groups. But we don't have those sorts of celebrations
for newer immigrants from places like Syria, Somalia,
or El Salvador.

"We were not brought here to be made citizens.
We were brought here against our will. We were
not brought here to enjoy the constitutional
gifts that they speak so beautifully about."

Malcolm X

According to the Census Bureau, there are about 3.8 million people in the United States who identify solely as American Indian and Alaska Native, about 1.2% of the US population. When Europeans first came to America, it is thought that roughly 10 million Native Peoples lived in the area that would become the United States.

Source: US Census Bureau

10 million
Native Peoples
in the U.S. when
Europeans first arived

3.8 million
identify today as
American Indian
or Alaska Native

Ethnic and racial groups with recognized commemorative months: Blacks, Greek-Americans, Irish-Americans, Asian-Pacific Americans, Jewish-Americans, Latinx people, German-Americans, Italian-Americans, Polish-Americans, and American Indians.

Source: Wake Forest University

WHAT YOU CAN DO

■ Attend a local festival or commemoration for an immigrant group to which you do not belong. Get to know one new person at the event, and ask that person his or her story.

■ Research the migration story of your family.

■ Find out which immigrant groups are present in your community. A good place to start is by looking up Pew Research Center demographic data. Then encourage your local and state government officials to pass commemorative legislation to honor those groups. See page 145 for a helpful guide on contacting your representatives.

During the trans-Atlantic slave trade (1525–1866), 12.5 million Africans were shipped to North America.

Source: The Root

REFLECTION & JOURNAL SPACE

■ Where have you heard the statement "We're all immigrants" before? Who said it? How did others respond?

■ How would you respond right now if someone said, "We're all immigrants"? What would you say in reply?

■ What did you learn about your family's migration story? How does that shape your identity?

ARE WE POST-RACIAL?

You might know . . .

The Civil Rights Act of 1964 outlawed discrimination based on race, color, religion, sex, or national origin.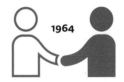

But maybe you've never thought about . . .

Systemic racism still exists in this country. Race is a social construct. It is deeply ingrained in our policies, laws, social practices, and resource allocation. People of color and indigenous communities continue to face discriminatory treatment and exclusion from access to equal opportunity. This shows up everywhere from education to health care, law and policy, and our everyday interactions with each other.

"For those of you who are tired of hearing about racism, imagine how much more tired we are of constantly experiencing it."

Barbara Smith, *The Truth That Never Hurts*

9% of white people in the United States are in poverty;
24% of Black people in the United States are in poverty;
21% of Latinx people in the United States are in poverty.
Source: Kaiser Family Foundation

White   Black   Latinx

Percent of U.S. population
in poverty by race

Recent data from the Bureau of Labor Statistics show
that the unemployment rate for white people is 4.3%,
the unemployment rate for Black people is 8.4%,
the unemployment rate for Latinx people is 5.8%,
and the unemployment rate for Asian people is 3.6%.
Source: Bureau of Labor Statistics

Latinx people make up 16% of the total US population
and 19% of the prison population. Native Peoples make
up less than 1% of the total US population and 1% of
the prison population.
Source: Prison Policy Initiative

WHAT YOU CAN DO

■ Read the newspaper and watch the evening news. Pay attention to how people of various races are described, and compare those descriptions.

■ Attend a racial-justice event or rally in your community as a listener. Pay attention to the stories being told there.

■ Ask your kids' teachers whether people of color are being represented in the books and curriculum resources used in their classrooms. Excellent resources can be found at the National Association for Multicultural Education (nameorg.org/learn).

■ Join a racial-justice advocacy group. See the helpful guide for choosing an organization to support on page 143.

White people make up 64% of the US population but only 39% of the prison population.
Black people make up only 13% of the US population but 40% of the prison population.

Source: Prison Policy Initiative

REFLECTION & JOURNAL SPACE

■ Have you described yourself or your community as post-racial? What does that mean? What does it ignore?

■ What stories did you hear at a racial-justice event? How did they affect your thinking about ongoing racial injustice?

■ How are people of color described and represented differently in the news? How does that affect your perceptions?

NATIVE LAND

You might know . . .

The United States was
built on land taken from
indigenous peoples.

But maybe you've never thought about . . .

The federal government is still taking land from
Native Peoples. Native Peoples do not own their
reservation lands. The lands are held in trust by
the federal government, giving Native Peoples little
control and making it impossible for them to leverage
their assets for loans and to promote economic
growth. Tribes and nations in the United States
fight constantly against the sale and seizure of their
remaining land, and dispossession goes hand in hand
with natural-resource exploitation. Native Peoples
stand on the front lines against hydraulic fracturing
and oil pipelines that threaten our environment and
contribute to climate change.

"Someone needs to explain to me why wanting
clean drinking water makes you an activist, and
why proposing to destroy water with chemical
warfare doesn't make a corporation a terrorist."

Winona LaDuke

Less than 3% of US land is designated for American Indians, Indian tribes, and Alaskan Natives.

Source: U.S. Geological Survey

2014

In 2014, two of the biggest international mining companies proposed to mine the copper ore under Oak Flat, an action that would have been impossible had Congress not approved the Southeast Arizona Land Exchange, which gave the companies rights to the once-protected land. Protesters continue to fight this issue on the grounds that mining would have negative environmental impacts and would defile land thought to be sacred by Native Peoples.

Source: Earthworks

WHAT YOU CAN DO

- Pay a visit to a reservation in or near your community. Many tribes have information for visitors on their websites, including information about events that are open to the public.

- Contact your federal representatives, and ask them to sponsor legislation that would allow Native Peoples to buy and sell reservation land for economic growth. See page 145 for a helpful guide to contacting your representatives.

- Contribute money to the Indian Land Tenure Foundation, and use the foundation's educational resources to inform yourself and your community.

Utah

According to the US Department of the Interior, approximately 55.7 million acres of land are designated for American Indians, Indian tribes, and Alaska Natives. If compiled, the land mass would be roughly the size of Utah.

Source: U.S. Geological Survey

REFLECTION & JOURNAL SPACE

■ What is the story of the land you live on? What Native Peoples inhabited it centuries ago, and what Native Peoples are present now?

■ Where does your clean drinking water come from? What Native Peoples are affected by that resource extraction?

WATER

You might know . . .

Access to clean water remains a problem around the world, even in some US locations, including Flint, Michigan.

But maybe you've never thought about . . .

Despite infrastructure and treatment facilities nationwide, hundreds of thousands of Americans lack access to clean drinking water, and tens of thousands have no water for sanitation. Most Americans receiving contaminated water are poor, rural, native, and immigrants living in border communities. Flint, Michigan, and Standing Rock Indian Reservation are just the latest conflicts in the ongoing water crisis the world faces.

....

"Water is life."

Standing Rock Dakota Access Pipeline (DAPL) protest

According to the World Health Organization, even blood lead concentrations as low as 5 milligrams per deciliter (that's very low!) can affect children's intelligence, behavior, and ability to learn. No safe blood lead level in children has been identified.

Source: World Health Organization

5 ml/dl

Almost 24,000 American Indian and Alaska Native households do not have access to running water or basic sanitation facilities, and the water and sanitation facilities of more than 188,000 of such households are in need of improvement.

Source: The New York Times

WHAT YOU CAN DO

■ Learn about and protect your own water. The Safe Drinking Water Act requires states to conduct assessments of water sources. Find out what your source is and how it measures up to others.

■ Take personal steps to protect your drinking water by reducing use of pesticides, toxic household cleaners, and other known contaminants.

■ The front lines in the water crisis are often scarcely populated and far from urban centers. Support the communities most affected by the water crisis—Native communities, immigrants, and the rural poor—with financial aid or gifts that are specifically requested.

The United States has approximately 1.2 million miles of lead pipes that are used for transporting water, and as they age, these pipes are slowly eroding into the water they carry.

Source: DeSmogBlog

REFLECTION & JOURNAL SPACE

- When was the last time you worried about the safety of the water coming out of your tap?

- For months, water protectors in North Dakota protested oil pipelines that threatened their water. Why do you think Native communities struggle to get clean water?

LGBTQIA EQUALITY

You might know . . .

Marriage equality is the law of the land in all fifty states.

But maybe you've never thought about . . .

Legal equality isn't the be-all and end-all of LGBTQIA (lesbian, gay, bisexual, transgender, queer, intersex, asexual) equity. Just because the law changes, that doesn't mean the culture changes along with it. There are no federal workplace protections for LGBTQIA people. LGBTQIA children are still being bullied in school and have no legal recourse. LGBTQIA parents are often barred from adoption. Anti-LGBTQIA stigma is one of the primary reasons that people avoid testing and treatment for HIV and AIDS. Many churches still reinforce discrimination in their preaching and policies, and religious freedom is used as a tool to sanction discrimination in public accommodation.

"It takes no compromise to give people their rights. . . . It takes no money to respect the individual. It takes no political deal to give people freedom. It takes no survey to remove repression."

Harvey Milk

5 states permit state-licensed child welfare agencies to not allow LGBT parents to adopt if doing so is contrary to the agency's religious beliefs.

Source: Family Equality Council

50

Number of states that allow LGBT parents to petition for joint adoption

7

Number of states with laws that specifically protect adoption rights based on parents' sexual orientation

3

Number of states with laws that specifically protect adoption rights based on parents' gender identity

A 2010 study found that approximately 47,500 new HIV cases had been reported in the United States. HIV rates among Latino and Black males were 2.5 and 6.5 times higher, respectively, than among white males.

Source: National Alliance of State and Territorial AIDS Directors

White		
Latino	2.5 x	
Black		6.5 x

Male HIV rates in 2010

WHAT YOU CAN DO

■ Read *It's Not Over: Getting Beyond Tolerance, Defeating Homophobia, and Winning True Equality*, by Michelangelo Signorile (Houghton Mifflin Harcourt, 2015).

■ Attend a Pride celebration in your community.

■ Find a local PFLAG chapter and attend a meeting. Be a listener and ask questions.

■ Talk with your LGBTQIA family members or to the people you know who have LGBTQIA children.

■ Invite an LGBTQIA speaker to your church, workplace, or community organization.

■ Find out if your church is welcoming for LGBTQIA people and whether you are communicating that welcome clearly.

As of this writing, only 19 states and the District of Columbia have specific nondiscrimination laws for people who are LGBTQIA.

Source: Human Rights Watch

REFLECTION & JOURNAL SPACE

■ Has your interest in or enthusiasm for promoting LGBTQIA rights changed since the Supreme Court ruled on Obergefell v. Hodges, legalizing same-sex marriage in 2015?

■ As you engaged in conversation and listened to LGBTQIA people, when did you feel uncomfortable?

■ How do the current legal challenges for LGBTQIA people (especially questions of religious freedom) echo racial discrimination from the past?

WHAT DO THE LETTERS MEAN?

The following definitions are derived from the Lesbian, Gay, Bisexual, Transgender, Queer, Intersex, Asexual Resource Center at the University of California, Davis.

■ *Lesbian* A woman whose sexual and affectional orientation is toward people of the same gender.

■ *Gay* A sexual and affectional orientation toward people of the same gender; can be used as an umbrella term for men and women.

■ *Bisexual* A person whose primary sexual and affectional orientation is toward people of the same and other genders or toward people regardless of their gender.

■ *Transgender* Adjective used most often as an umbrella term and frequently abbreviated to trans. It describes a wide range of identities and experiences of people whose gender identity and/or expression differs from conventional expectations based on their assigned sex at birth. Not all trans people undergo medical transition (surgery or hormones).

■ *Queer* One definition of queer is abnormal or strange. Some have reclaimed the term as a celebration of not fitting into norms and use queer as a radical and anti-assimilationist stance that captures multiple aspects of identities.

■ *Intersex*   People who naturally (that is, without any medical intervention) develop primary or secondary sex characteristics that do not fit neatly into society's definitions of male or female.

■ *Asexual*   A sexual orientation generally characterized by not feeling sexual attraction or a desire for partnered sexuality. Asexuality is distinct from celibacy, which is the deliberate abstention from sexual activity. Some asexual people do have sex.

■ *Cisgender*   A gender identity, or performance in a gender role, that society deems to match the person's assigned sex at birth. The prefix cis- means "on this side of" or "not across." The term is used to call attention to the privilege of people who are not transgender.

ABLEISM

You might know . . .

People living with disabilities
face unique challenges as they
move through the world.

But maybe you've never thought about . . .

Ableism is a set of practices and beliefs that assign
inferior value and worth to persons with disabilities.
We often lift up perfect health as an ideal and disability
as a tragedy to overcome—even going so far as to screen
our children before birth for certain "defects." But health
is not a single state of the body. Instead, health is the
vitality to live with change and adapt to the unexpected.
Far more than medical and technological advancements
aimed at "rehabilitation," what is most needed is a shift
in our thinking about disability. We ought to think of
disability advocacy not in terms of medical rehabilitation,
but as an issue of civil rights—advocating for greater
support and access for persons with disabilities.

"The people who seem most hostile to my
presence are those most fearful of my fate. And
since their fear keeps them emotionally distant
from me, they are the ones least likely to learn
that my life isn't half so dismal as they assume."

Nancy Mairs, *Waist-High in the World*

1840

The word *normal*, meaning common or standard, didn't enter the English language until around 1840. Before that time, the concept of an ideal human body would have only occurred in myths.

1981

The term *ableism* was first officially used in 1981 to describe the preferential treatment of a society toward able-bodied people and against persons with disabilities.

Many conditions can be screened for before a child is born, such as Down syndrome, spina bifida, some chromosomal abnormalities, some physical defects, cystic fibrosis, muscular dystrophy, fragile X syndrome, haemophilia (a blood clot disorder), and thalassaemia (a blood disorder). The morality of such screenings is hotly contested, and the prevalence of screening is one manifestation of ableist attitudes.

Source: Women's and Children's Health Network

WHAT YOU CAN DO

■ Use people-first language (person living with autism, person living with cancer, etc.). Stop using ableist words like crazy, insane, or retarded.

■ Watch the film *The Intouchables* with your friends or coworkers, and host a discussion afterward.

■ Identify ableist assumptions in the places you occupy: your workplace, your church, your school.

There is no living body that actually fits the "statistical norm."

REFLECTION & JOURNAL SPACE

■ Who do you know that is living with a disability? What unique perspective and ability does that person bring to your community?

■ Where and how does our culture's preference for perfect health (especially our fixation on medical and technological advancement) play against persons with disabilities, making them stand out as different?

■ How can you welcome alternative hopes and dreams for your current or future children outside the framework of perfect health?

WHITE SUPREMACY

You might know . . .

The Southern Poverty Law Center and the Anti-Defamation League designate white supremacist organizations as hate groups.

But maybe you've never thought about . . .

"White supremacy" does not only refer to white supremacist groups. White supremacy is a deeply embedded cultural imagination that assumes whiteness is the norm or the universal, and every white person benefits from it. It is ingrained in our pop culture and media, our religious institutions, our educational institutions, our businesses, our government, and even our language. White fragility is the distress white people experience when even a small amount of racial strain occurs, triggering defensiveness.

....

"In this country, American means white. Everybody else has to hyphenate."

Toni Morrison

Median household income for white people is $62,950, as compared with $45,148 for Latinx people and $36,898 for Black people.
Source: Statista

The median net worth of white households is 13 times higher than that of Black households and 10 times greater than that of Latinx households.
Source: Pew Research Center

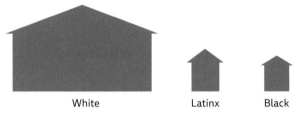

White   Latinx   Black

Median household net worth

Actors of color cast in movie franchises traditionally dominated by white characters have been met with significant backlash. Recent examples include Michael B. Jordan playing Johnny Storm in the newest *Fantastic Four* movie and John Boyega playing a stormtrooper in *The Force Awakens*.

> ■ *Microaggression* Brief and commonplace daily verbal, behavioral, or environmental indignities, whether intentional or unintentional, that communicate hostile, derogatory, or negative slights and insults about one's marginalized identity/identities.

WHAT YOU CAN DO

■ Pay attention to the ways that white culture appropriates and tokenizes people of color and Native Peoples for entertainment. Seek out credible movies, books, and television shows that represent the experiences of people of color and Native Peoples.

■ Take the Harvard implicit-bias test at <u>implicit.harvard.edu</u>.

■ Use your privilege to advocate on behalf of anti-racist policies and practices. Name white supremacy when you see it in the community and institutions you're a part of.

■ Start a book group on the topic of racial justice. Begin with these two books: *Post Traumatic Slave Syndrome* by Joy DeGruy Leary (Uptone, 2005) and *Between the World and Me* by Ta-Nehisi Coates (Spiegel & Grau, 2015).

■ Attend an event hosted by people of color (a poetry reading, a community event, worship at a Black church). Have authentic conversations with people of color, and expose yourself to people from diverse communities.

People

Halle Berry was the first person of color to be named *People* magazine's Most Beautiful Person, in 2003.

REFLECTION & JOURNAL SPACE

- ■ Make a list of ten ways you benefit from and contribute to systems of white supremacy.

- ■ What was it like to push yourself out of your comfort zone and attend an event hosted by people of color? What was most uncomfortable about the experience? What did you learn?

- ■ When have you experienced white fragility in yourself or witnessed it in others?

LIFE FOR NATIVE PEOPLES

You might know . . .

Many Native Peoples
live on reservations.

But maybe you've never thought about . . .

Life for Native Peoples is profoundly shaped by a history
of mass murder, genocide, and slavery imposed by
European colonizers. Native communities today face
high rates of poverty and unemployment. Inadequate
federal funding leads to drastically low graduation
rates, deteriorating schools, substandard housing,
poor health care, and lack of support for cultural
preservation. Native Peoples—especially Native women
and children—suffer from an epidemic of violence, and
often this violence comes from outside the community.
It is important to note, however, that many Native
Peoples do not live on reservations, and that Native
communities are found in US cities and towns as well
and face unique challenges in those settings.

"In Iroquois society, leaders are encouraged to
remember seven generations in the past and
consider seven generations in the future when
making decisions that affect the people."

Wilma Mankiller, the first woman elected
to serve as chief of the Cherokee Nation

The high school graduation rate for American Indians and
Alaska Natives was 72% in 2014–15, almost 10 percentage
points below the national average.

Source: National Center for Educational Statistics

72

American Indian and Alaska Native women are 2.5 times
more likely to experience sexual assault than the general US
population; 86% of those who commit sexually violent crimes
against Native persons are of another race.

Source: Washington Coalition of Sexual Health Programs

Native Women

US Population

Relative likelihood of experiencing sexual assault

WHAT YOU CAN DO

■ Spend your money at Native-owned businesses. Visit the website of the American Indian Business Alliance to search for businesses in your community.

■ A resolution to designate May 5 as National Day of Awareness for Missing and Murdered Native Women and Girls was introduced to Congress in April 2016. Contact your representatives and urge them to support the resolution. Wear red on May 5, and attend or host a prayer vigil or other community event on that day.

■ Advocate with your state and federal representatives for more funding to be directed to American Indians and Alaska Natives. See page 145 for a helpful guide to contacting your representatives.

26

The poverty rate for American Indians and Alaska Natives is 26%.

Source: Pew Research Center

REFLECTION & JOURNAL SPACE

■   Who are the Native communities in your area?
    What have you learned about their history?

■   Who are the Native women and girls missing in
    or near your community? What are their stories?

SEXUAL VIOLENCE

You might know . . .

One out of every five women has been the victim of sexual assault.

But maybe you've never thought about . . .

Sexual violence is a broad term that refers to more than just intercourse without consent. Sexual violence also includes threatening remarks, sexual harassment, voyeurism, unwanted touching, and human trafficking, among other acts. Children and people of color are particularly vulnerable to sexual violence—especially Native American women. Sexual violence is the least reported crime, and victims of sexual violence are often blamed for their own abuse by their families and by law enforcement.

"Support. Listen. Take action. Not because she's someone's daughter, or someone's girlfriend, or someone's sister, but because she is someone."

Cast of HBO's *Girls*

1 in 5 women and 1 in 71 men in the US have experienced rape or attempted rape. The percentage of women raped during their lifetimes is 32% for multiracial women, 28% for American Indian/Alaska Native women, 21% for Black women, 21% for white women, and 14% for Latina women.

| Multiracial | American Indian/ Alaska Native | Black | White | Latina |

Percent of women who have experienced rape or attempted rape

Almost 74% of adolescents who have been sexually assaulted were victimized by someone they knew well. 21.1% of those assaults were committed by a family member.
Source: National Sexual Violence Resource Center

The highest-risk years for rape and sexual assault are ages 12 to 34.

Sexual violence can have long-term effects on victims. Among women who have been raped, 94% experience post-traumatic stress disorder following the rape; 33% of women who have been raped contemplate taking their own lives, and 13% attempt to take their own lives.
Source: RAINN

There are an estimated 20.9 million victims of human trafficking globally. In 2016, an estimated 1 out of 6 endangered runaways were likely child-sex-trafficking victims.
Source: Polaris Project

WHAT YOU CAN DO

- Share the National Sexual Assault Hotline with a friend or loved one. Call 800-656-HOPE or visit hotline.rainn.org.

- Look for enthusiastic and affirmative consent, not the abence of consent, with your romantic partners. Instead of a "no means no" mentality, change to a "yes means yes" mentality. Teach the children and young people in your life that only they can decide what happens with their body.

- April is Sexual Assault Awareness Month (SAAM). Visit the website of the National Sexual Violence Resource Center (nsvrc.org) to learn more about the history of SAAM and to plan a campaign for your community this April.

- Check with the schools and universities in your community about their sexual-violence policies, and advocate for more consent education and better protection and empowerment for survivors.

Among women who have been sexually assaulted, 12.3% were age ten or younger at the time of their first rape/victimization, and 30% were between the ages of eleven and seventeen.

REFLECTION & JOURNAL SPACE

■ It is likely that you already know a survivor of sexual assault or that you are a survivor yourself. Whose story do you know that has affected you?

■ How can you change from a "no means no" mind-set to a "yes means yes" mind-set when thinking about consent, both in terms of your own sexuality and when teaching the young people in your life?

TRANSGENDER EQUALITY

You might know . . .

Trans people are becoming more visible in the media.

But maybe you've never thought about . . .

Most trans people don't have the same platform and visibility as, for example, Caitlyn Jenner or Laverne Cox. For many trans people, there is risk in visibility, and not every trans person "passes" for their gender identity in the same way. Trans people are disproportionately victims of violence and discrimination, especially trans women of color. Trans people are more likely to be fired, refused medical care, and refused recognition by government agencies. There is no perfect model for transition or gender presentation.

"It is revolutionary for any trans person to choose to be seen and visible in a world that tells us we should not exist."

Laverne Cox

As of summer 2017, 16 states have proposed adopting "bathroom bills": legislation for multiuser bathrooms, locker rooms, and other facilities requiring persons to use the facility corresponding to the sex assigned to them at birth, regardless of their gender identity.

Source: National Conference of State Legislatures

Of the LGBT murder victims in 2011, 87% were people of color. Of hate murders committed, 45% of the victims were transgender women.

Source: Gay and Lesbian Alliance Against Defamation

Approximately 41% of transgender people attempt to take their own lives at some point. About 45% of that number were between the ages of eighteen and twenty-four when they attempted suicide.

Source: Williams Institute, UCLA School of Law

WHAT YOU CAN DO

■ When you meet people, ask them what pronouns they prefer to use. Redesign documents used by your workplace, church, or organization so that they don't assume a gender binary.

■ Educate yourself about the differences between sex, sexuality, gender identity, and gender expression. Suggest that your workplace, church, or community group adopt a curriculum about gender diversity to learn more.

■ Pay attention to the way you talk about gender and gender roles, especially with the children in your life. Work to dismantle your assumptions that rely on gender-binary norms.

■ Find out if your workplace has a nondiscrimination policy protecting trans people. If not, put one in place, including protections for use of restrooms.

■ Attend an antidiscrimination rally held by the National Center for Transgender Equality, the National LGBTQ Task Force, Human Rights Campaign, or another organization dedicated to transgender rights.

■ If you are the parent of a trans child, be in contact with your school about how they can support your child. Know your rights and seek legal counsel whenever you encounter barriers.

REFLECTION & JOURNAL SPACE

■   What pronouns do you prefer to be called? What does it feel like to share your pronouns and ask others to share theirs?

■   How does your gender inform your sense of self? What assumptions do you make about others based on their gender expression?

SOME HELPFUL DEFINITIONS

The following definitions are from the Lesbian, Gay, Bisexual, Transgender, Queer, Intersex, Asexual Resource Center at the University of California, Davis.

- *Sex* A medically constructed categorization. Sex is often assigned based on the appearance of the genitalia, either in ultrasound or at birth.

- *Sexuality* The components of a person that include their biological sex, sexual orientation, gender identity, sexual practices, etc.

- *Gender identity* A sense of one's self as trans, genderqueer, woman, man, or some other identity, which may or may not correspond with the sex and gender one is assigned at birth.

- *Gender expression* How one expresses oneself, in terms of dress and/or behaviors. Society and people who make up society characterize these expressions as "masculine," "feminine," or "androgynous." Individuals may embody their gender in a multitude of ways and have terms beyond these to name their gender expression(s).

THE GENDER WAGE GAP

You might know . . .

Women are paid about 80 cents for every dollar a man makes.

But maybe you've never thought about . . .

That common statistic is based only on the wages of educated white women. When we talk about the wage gap, we need to make sure we are thinking about the impact of wage discrepancies for all women, especially women of color. When you say "women," remind yourself to ask who is included and who isn't.

"Their goal wasn't to stand out because of their differences; it was to fit in because of their talents. Like the men they worked for, and the men they sent hurtling off into the atmosphere, they were just doing their jobs."

Margot Lee Shetterly, *Hidden Figures: The Untold True Story of Four African-American Women Who Helped Launch Our Nation into Space*

Women of all races earn 78.3% of what men of all races earn.

78

	COMPARED TO WHITE MEN	COMPARED TO MEN OF SAME RACE

Latina women earn 54% of what white men earn and 90% of what Latino men earn.

54   90

American Indian and Alaskan Native Women earn 59% of what white men earn and 85% of what American Indian and Alaskan Native men earn.

59   85

African American women earn 64% of what white men earn and 91% of what black men earn.

64   91

Asian American women earn 90% of what white men earn, and 79% of what Asian American men earn.

90   79

White women earn 76% of what white men earn.

76

Sources: Census Bureau current population survey and 2013 American community survey

WHAT YOU CAN DO

▪ Start using more accurate statistics when you talk or post about this issue, and point others to the stats when they speak about the issue in general terms.

▪ Know your rights. Read about the Lilly Ledbetter Fair Pay Act of 2009 on the website of the Equal Employment Opportunity Commission (EEOC). Encourage your employer to look over their wage policies. Review your own pay, and encourage coworkers to do the same.

▪ Find out if your state has voted to ratify the ERA. If not, contact your representatives (see page 145 for a helpful guide to contacting your representatives), and ask them to reintroduce it.

▪ Hold a fund-raiser in your community benefiting an organization that supports women; see page 143 for a helpful guide to choosing an organization to support. Ask women to pay 54 percent of the listed price (the lowest stat), and keep the stats visible.

1972

The Equal Rights Amendment was first introduced in 1972 and has yet to be ratified.

REFLECTION & JOURNAL SPACE

- How did it feel to talk with your employer or coworkers about wages? Did any insecurity or fear arise?

- Has the pay gap pushed you toward or away from any particular opportunities?

EQUALITY AND EQUITY

You might know ...

Affirmative action was
implemented to ensure
equal access for everyone.

But maybe you've never thought about ...

Affirmative action mostly benefits white women.
Equality does not equal equity. We like to think
about equality, which assumes we all start from the
same place and with the same chance for success.
Equity, in contrast, recognizes that race, ethnicity,
educational background, and socioeconomic status
all play a role in a person's ability to achieve success;
we don't all start from the same place. Equity is a
commitment to removing barriers and creating
equal access to opportunities.

"For to be free is not merely to cast off one's
chains, but to live in a way that respects and
enhances the freedom of others."

Nelson Mandela, *Long Walk to Freedom*

The Department of Labor estimated that 6 million white women workers are in higher occupational classifications today than they would have been without affirmative action policies.

Source: Racism Review

The unemployment rate for white women is 7.2%, compared with 13.3% for Black women and 11.4% for Latina women.

Source: Center for American Progress

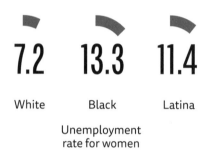

7.2	13.3	11.4
White	Black	Latina

Unemployment
rate for women

According to the American Civil Liberties Union, 17 states have implemented various voter suppression laws, including required voter IDs, dual registration systems, and early-voting cutbacks. These laws disproportionately affect people of color and persons living with disabilities.

Source: American Civil Liberties Union

WHAT YOU CAN DO

■ Look around your workplace. Who is represented? If you are making hiring decisions, take a look at your hiring criteria and whether they create a barrier, especially for people of color. If you don't make hiring decisions, encourage your employers to evaluate their criteria.

■ Look around your community. Are people of color present in your church, on your sports team, in your kids' school? If not, ask why. Consider the benefits of surrounding yourself with a more diverse group of people.

■ Contact your representatives to advocate for voting rights protections, particularly if voter ID laws or other voting restriction laws are proposed. See page 145 for a helpful guide on contacting your representatives.

Equality

Equity

REFLECTION & JOURNAL SPACE

■ A commitment to equity, rather than equality, might mean giving up your own resources or opportunities to make space for others. Does this feel fair to you? If not, ask yourself why.

■ Who do you see represented in your workplace and community? What is the value of surrounding yourself with people who are unlike you?

■ Which of your successes are you most proud of? Make a list of the support systems and advantages that helped you achieve that success.

NATIVE PEOPLES' RIGHTS

You might know . . .

Native Peoples are a protected class under Title VII, which prohibits discrimination based on race or color.

But maybe you've never thought about . . .

Many have never received federal recognition. Lack of recognition means that Native communities have less or little access to legal protection, economic opportunities, social services, and the ability to preserve their culture. Native Peoples face barriers to voting. Tens of thousands of Native voters have to travel miles to the nearest polling place, and many reservations do not have access to early voting. They make such a small voting bloc that their influence is very limited. Nonnative allies are needed to make an impact, especially in the political sphere.

"Know that you yourself are essential to this world. Understand both the blessing and the burden of that. You yourself are desperately needed to save the soul of this world. Did you think you were put here for something less?"

Chief Arvol Looking Horse

The Duck Valley Reservation in Nevada is 104 miles away from the nearest polling place, located in Elko, Nevada (about a two-hour drive). The Goshute Reservation in Utah in 163 miles away from the nearest polling place, located in Erda, Utah (almost a three-hour drive).

Source: Native News Online

Duck Valley Reservation

Elko, NV

104 miles

Erda, UT

163 miles

Goshute Reservation

2015

The Tribal Equal Access to Voting Act of 2015 was meant to help curb the difficulties and inequalities Native Peoples faced regarding voting. The Native American Voting Rights Act of 2015 was meant to protect the voting rights of Native Peoples by preventing states from imposing unfair or unequal standards on tribal polling places and by improving Native Peoples' access to polling places. Both bills have stalled in Congress.

WHAT YOU CAN DO

■ Research the past and present Native communities in your area, and find out if they are legally recognized. Advocate for quicker and easier paths for legal recognition for Native Peoples.

■ Contact your state and federal representatives and ask them to sponsor legislation to ensure access to voting for American Indians and Alaska Natives. See page 145 for a helpful guide on contacting your representatives.

■ Contact or research the Native communities in your area before you vote each Election Day, and when you cast your ballot, prioritize the issues and concerns they identify.

700

More than 700 American Indian and Alaska Native tribes and groups remain unrecognized by the federal government.

Source: World Heritage Encyclopedia

REFLECTION & JOURNAL SPACE

■ What opportunities and protections are afforded to you
by your legal status (if applicable)?

■ What is your experience of voting? Consider the barriers
you do and don't face, and compare them to the barriers
faced by many Native peoples.

WOMEN IN GOVERNMENT

You might know . . .

Congress now has more
women than ever.

But maybe you've never thought about . . .

The United States is still far from equal when it
comes to representation of women in government,
lagging behind much of the rest of the world. Rates of
representation for women of color are far lower than
those for white women. Many women in government
experience harassment, physical violence, and sexual
violence, and we treat women candidates and leaders
with far greater scrutiny—from the way they dress to
whether they seem "nice"—than male candidates.

....

"A woman's place is in the House...
and the Senate."

Of the 104 women serving in the 115th US Congress, 38 or 36.5%, are women of color. Women of color constitute 7.1% of the total 535 members of Congress.

Women hold 3 of the 9 seats on the Supreme Court.

Women hold 24.9% of state legislature seats.

Women of color constitute 5.9% of state legislators and 23.7% of women state legislators.

20

Of the 100 largest cities in the United States, 20% have women mayors. 8 of those 100 are women of color.
Source: Rutgers University, Center for American Women and Politics

The United States ranks number 101 among other nations in terms of the percentage of women representatives. Rwanda is ranked number one, with women holding 61% of lower-house seats and 38% of upper-house seats. Pakistan and Bangladesh both rank ahead of the United States, with women holding around 20% of seats.
Source: Inter-Parliamentary Union

Women representatives in the lower house by %

WHAT YOU CAN DO

- Find out how many women are serving in your local and state governments.

- Support a female candidate for office by donating to or volunteering for her campaign.

- Research local and national groups that are helping women run for office, and support them with your dollars and your vote.

- Research the first woman to represent your congressional district, the first woman to serve as mayor of your city, or the first woman to hold another important office in your community. Share her story with your family and friends.

Women hold 19.4% of the 535 seats in the US Congress. They hold 21% of the 100 seats of the US Senate and 19.1% of the 435 seats in the House of Representatives.

REFLECTION & JOURNAL SPACE

■ What women leaders, past or present, inspire you most?

■ Do you expect different behavior from female leaders?
If you do, ask yourself why.

■ How do you see female leaders unfairly judged in their roles?

CONTRIBUTIONS OF IMMIGRANTS

You might know . . .

Immigrants positively affect our economy.

But maybe you've never thought about . . .

The image some people use to talk about immigrants and our economy is a pie. Many fear that when immigrants enter the job market, they'll take up pieces of the pie that "should" belong to other Americans. The reality, however, is that the pie itself gets bigger when more immigrants join our job force, because they help our economy grow. Furthermore, anti-immigration policies put us at risk of losing valuable contributions to our economy and society. Immigrants with the most in-demand skills (like technology and medicine) have the means to leave the United States if our public policy and culture don't support them.

"Immigrants are exactly what America needs. They help our country tremendously. They help us with the work they do. . . . They challenge us with new ideas, and with new perspectives."

Rudy Giuliani

Immigrants started 28% of all new U.S. businesses in 2011, despite accounting for just 12.9% of the U.S. population.

Source: Partnership for a New Economy

New business starts	US Population

Percent Immigrants

Many well-known companies in the United States were started by immigrants; examples include Google, Yahoo, Colgate, AT&T, eBay, and Kraft. In fact, immigrants are more than twice as likely to start a business as someone born in America.

Source: Huffington Post

US Natives

US Immigrants

Likelihood of starting a business

WHAT YOU CAN DO

- Pay attention to where you shop, who your doctor is, and who you hire to do work in your business or on your home. Seek out and patronize the businesses of new immigrants whenever possible.

- Contact leaders in your place of employment, your child's school, or your local government, and ask them to seek out new immigrants when they are hiring for new positions.

- Do some research about immigrants who have made a significant impact on our economy, such as Sergey Brin and Jerry Yang.

14.7

A 2012 study by the Economic Policy Institute reports that immigrants contributed roughly 14.7% of the United States' economic output from 2009 to 2011.

Source: Economic Policy Institute

REFLECTION & JOURNAL SPACE

■ How do you define our identity as a nation? What does it mean to be an "American"?

■ Do you notice a feeling of scarcity (a feeling that there won't be enough pie for everyone) when you think about how immigrants affect the job market? Has your actual experience reinforced that feeling or challenged it?

■ What was it like to patronize the businesses of new immigrants? What do you gain from their presence in your community?

BULLYING OF LGBTQIA YOUTH

You might know . . .

Young people are coming
out earlier as our culture
has become more accepting
of LGBTQIA people.

But maybe you've never thought about . . .

Young LGBTQIA people are especially vulnerable to
bullying and abuse. Negative stereotypes, hateful
language, abusive theology, and discriminatory policies
are still prevalent. These messages have a lasting and
profound impact on young people, who are still in the
process of determining their own identity. Churches
espousing a "love the sinner, hate the sin" approach
reinforce self-hatred and separation between families—
the very people who ought to be supporting young
people the most. Young people who don't have the
support of their families are particularly vulnerable to
abuse, exploitation, and homelessness.

"The greatest gift you ever
give is your honest self."

Fred Rogers

Among students who identified as LGBTQIA, 82% said they experienced bullying about sexual orientation, and almost 60% never reported what happened to them.

Teenagers who identify as LGBTQIA are 2 to 3 times more likely to attempt to take their own lives than their peers are; they are 8 times more likely to take their own lives if they are not accepted by their family.

28% of youth who are LGBTQIA will stop going to school altogether because of the bullying they experience.

Source: NoBullying.com

Approximately 40% of youth experiencing homelessness identify as being LGBTQIA.

Source: Lambda Legal

WHAT YOU CAN DO

- Ask your local school board whether they have bullying policies in place, with specific protection for LGBTQIA kids.

- If you have children of your own, have conversations with them about bullying in school.

- Use the Trevor Project's Lifeguard Training (a free online video) with the kids in your school, church, sports team, or other community group.

- Pay attention to the media you consume and how those shows and movies portray LGBTQIA people. Give the young people in your life resources that represent LGBTQIA people well.

- Advocate for the formation of a Gay-Straight Alliance (GSA) in your local school. Human Rights Campaign has excellent resources for starting a GSA.

- If you are a parent of an LGBTQIA kid, look to PFLAG for helpful resources on how to support your child.

Students who identify as LGBTQIA will skip school 5 times more often than other students, due to the bullying they experience.

Source: NoBullying.com

REFLECTION & JOURNAL SPACE

- ■ What are your fears and your hopes for the kids in your life?

- ■ Were you bullied as a child? What helped you heal from that experience?

MENTAL HEALTH

You might know . . .

Mental health is a major problem in the United States.

But maybe you've never thought about . . .

When publicly funded mental health institutions were shut down—in a process known as deinstitutionalization, which took place in the 1970s—jails and prisons increasingly became surrogate mental hospitals for many people with severe mental-health issues. A shocking proportion of incarcerated people experience mental-health issues, and jails and prisons have very limited resources to provide adequate care. There is a direct correlation between mental-health issues and chemical dependency, further exacerbating this problem.

"We must stop criminalizing mental illness. It's a national tragedy and scandal that the L.A. County Jail is the biggest psychiatric facility in the United States."

Elyn Saks

The number of institutionalized individuals with mental illness dropped from 560,000 in 1950 to 130,000 in 1980.
Source: Unite for Sight

State funding for mental health is decreasing. The percentage of overall mental health spending contributed by states decreased between 1990 and 2009, from 27% to 15%.
Source: Pew Charitable Trusts

27
Percentage of mental health spending contributed by states
15

1990   2009

Of the youth incarcerated in juvenile justice systems, 70% have at least one mental-health condition, and about 20% suffer from serious mental-health issues.
Source: The National Center for Mental Health and Juvenile Justice

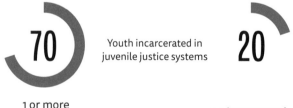

70
Youth incarcerated in juvenile justice systems
20

1 or more mental health conditions

serious mental health issues

WHAT YOU CAN DO

- Pay attention to the way people with mental-health issues are portrayed. Educate yourself and your community to remove the public stigma around mental illness.

- Contact your local representatives to advocate for funding and programs aimed at treating and assisting people with mental-health issues, especially those in jails and prisons. Advocate for more resources to be devoted to treatment, as opposed to incarceration. See page 145 for a helpful guide to contacting your representatives.

Among those with a serious mental illness, 23% also have a substance use disorder.

Source: Substance Abuse and Mental Health Services Administration

REFLECTION & JOURNAL SPACE

■   Who do you know in your family or community who lives with mental illness? What supports are in place for that person? What supports are still needed?

■   Why is it easier to fund incarceration of people with mental illness than to fund treatment and support?

WOMEN IN POVERTY

You might know . . .

Around 15 percent of Americans
live at or below the poverty line.

But maybe you've never thought about . . .

Poverty rates for women are higher than for men,
and women of color experience the highest rates
of poverty. Women are paid less than men for
equal work and are often segregated into lower-
paying work. Women are more likely to bear the
cost of raising children and caring for aging family
members. Women experience higher rates of sexual
and physical abuse, which can push them into a cycle
of poverty and incarceration. In fact, women are the
fastest-growing segment of the prison population.
Most of these women lived at or below the poverty
line before their incarceration. Many incarcerated
women are mothers of children under the age of
eighteen, and these children face higher rates of
mental-health issues and trauma.

"Poverty has a woman's face."

Tahira Abdullah

10% of men in the United States are in poverty, compared with 14% of women.

Source: Kaiser Family Foundation

Women of color experience higher rates of poverty than white women—specifically, 23% of African American women, 23% of Native women, 21% of Latina women, and 12% of Asian American women, versus 10% of white women.

| African American | Native | Latina | Asian America | White |

US poverty rate for women

Almost 56% of children experiencing poverty live in families led by single mothers.

Source: National Women's Law Center

More than 60% of women incarcerated in state prisons have children who are under the age of eighteen.

Source: Pew Research Center

WHAT YOU CAN DO

■ Encourage your employer to hire qualified women and to advocate for policies of flexible work and paid family leave to help women support their families.

■ Fund and support organizations, like Planned Parenthood, that give women living in poverty more control over their reproductive health.

■ Read *Killing the Black Body: Race, Reproduction, and the Meaning of Liberty*, by Dr. Dorothy Roberts and *Poster Child: The Kemba Smith Story*, by Kemba Smith with Monique W. Morris.

■ Contact your state and federal representatives to advocate for better care for pregnant women who are incarcerated, better protections for their children, and more programs in female prisons for mothers to be able to spend time with their children.

■ Advocate for comprehensive bail reform to reduce or eliminate the use of money bail. Donate to bail funds, especially for incarcerated mothers.

In 2013, approximately 2.7 million children (or about 1 in 18 children) had a parent who was incarcerated.

Source: Pew Research Center

REFLECTION & JOURNAL SPACE

- How has the burden of caregiving affected your life, if you are a woman, or the lives of the women in your family?

- What have you learned about the impact on children and families of incarcerated people, particularly women?

PRISON INDUSTRIAL COMPLEX

You might know ...

Operating prisons in the
United States is very expensive.

But maybe you've never thought about ...

Many private corporations benefit from mass
incarceration. The number of private prisons has
increased significantly, and these facilities have less
government oversight and greater risk of harm to
inmates. Prison companies' stocks are traded on
Wall Street for significant profit, and inmate labor
is used to benefit corporations and take jobs out of
our economy. There is a business incentive to keep
prisons open and filled.

"[Prison] relieves us of the responsibility of
seriously engaging with the problems of our
society, especially those produced by racism
and, increasingly, global capitalism."

Angela Davis, *Are Prisons Obsolete?*

Private prisons make approximately $374 million a year in profits.
Source: Prison Policy Initiative

The comprehensive mass incarceration system costs approximately $182 billion per year to operate.
Source: Prison Policy Initiative

Incarcerated people spend $1.6 billion each year on commissary necessities.
Source: Prison Policy Initiative

In one study, 65% of the private prisons analyzed had occupancy guarantees of 80–100% or compensatory fees for empty prison beds written into their contracts with states.
Source: In the Public Interest

Prisoners who participate in correctional education programs are roughly 43% less likely to return to prison and 13% more likely to find employment after their release.
Source: RAND Corporation

43 Prisoners who participate in education programs **13**

less likely
to return

more likely to find
employment

WHAT YOU CAN DO

■ Read *Are Prisons Obsolete?* by Angela Davis.

■ Find out which corporations in your state are investing in prisons, and actively avoid supporting those businesses with your dollars.

■ Research the prison industries in your state, and raise your concerns about those industries with state lawmakers. See page 145 for a helpful guide to contacting your representatives.

Phone calls cost incarcerated people
and their families $1.3 billion per year.

Source: Prison Policy Initiative

REFLECTION & JOURNAL SPACE

■   What products and services do you regularly consume from
     companies that profit from the prison industrial complex?

■   Where might your money be better invested if you divested
     from those companies?

WAR ON DRUGS

You might know ...

The government has taken a hard-line stance on drugs since the 1980s.

But maybe you've never thought about ...

The war on drugs intentionally targets people of color. Drug enforcement is not equitably applied: some drugs are criminalized more than others, and communities of color are policed more heavily than their white counterparts. Drug use in the United States has actually *increased* since the beginning of the war on drugs, all while the number of incarcerated people has increased dramatically.

"The fate of millions of people—indeed the future of the black community itself—may depend on the willingness of those who care about racial justice to re-examine their basic assumptions about the role of the criminal justice system in our society."

Michelle Alexander, *The New Jim Crow*

About one in five of those who are incarcerated, about 500,000 people total, are in jail or prison due to a drug-related offense.

16% of state prisoners, 50% of federal prisoners, 25% of those in jail, and 6% of youth in juvenile detention facilities are booked for drug-related offenses.

Source: Prison Policy Initiative

| State | Federal | Jail | Juvenile |

Percent of prisoners booked
for drug-related offenses

5x

White people use drugs at rates 5 times higher than African Americans.

Source: NAACP

10x

African Americans serve prison time for drug offenses at rates 10 times higher than white people.

WHAT YOU CAN DO

- Take steps to learn about the war on drugs and its history. A good place to start is the book *The New Jim Crow: Mass Incarceration in the Age of Colorblindness*, by Michelle Alexander (New Press, 2012).

- Contact your local and state representatives to advocate for decriminalization of low-level drug possession, and advocate for more equitable treatment within the justice system for drug offenders. See page 145 for a helpful guide to contacting your representatives.

- Advocate for drug treatment courts and more holistic approaches to solving the drug epidemic. Visit the website of the National Association of Drug Court Professionals at nadcp.org to learn whether drug courts exist in your jurisdiction and how to support their growth.

African Americans spend almost as much time in prison for drug-related offenses as white people do for violent offenses.

Source: NAACP

REFLECTION & JOURNAL SPACE

■ Do you tend to want punishment of drug users or treatment
for drug users? What values do you hold that lead you to prefer
one or the other?

■ How might you reframe your thinking about the criminal
justice system to be more about making the community whole
than about separating out and punishing certain members
of the community?

RACE AND INCARCERATION

You might know . . .

Mass incarceration is a major problem in the United States.

But maybe you've never thought about . . .

People of color are overrepresented in the criminal justice system. Racial stereotyping, racial profiling, and a high concentration of police in communities of color all contribute to a higher percentage of people of color cycling in and out of the criminal justice system. Greater rates of poverty in communities of color lead to survival crimes. Collateral consequences—such as employers refusing to hire and landlords refusing to rent to people with a criminal history, as well as the denial of public benefits—exacerbate the problem and create cycles of disadvantage.

"So many aspects of the old Jim Crow are suddenly legal again once you've been branded a felon. And so it seems that in America we haven't so much ended racial caste, but simply redesigned it."

Michelle Alexander

In the United States, almost 693 people in every 100,000 (or about 1 in 144) are incarcerated.

Source: The Prison Policy Initiative

Black people are incarcerated at significantly higher rates (1 in 43) than Latinx people (1 in 134) and white people (1 in 242).

Source: The Sentencing Project

1 in 43
Black

1 in 134
Latinx

1 in 242
White

The incarceration rate in the United States greatly surpasses other countries. For example, Russia (which has the sixth-highest rate) incarcerates 1 in 220 people, and India (which has one of the lowest rates) incarcerates 1 in 3,030 people.

Source: The Prison Policy Initiative

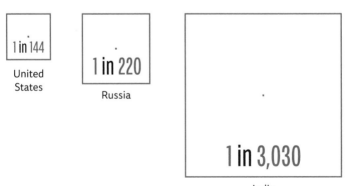

1 in 144
United States

1 in 220
Russia

1 in 3,030
India

WHAT YOU CAN DO

■ Educate yourself about mass incarceration. You can start by reading *Slavery by Another Name: The Re-enslavement of Black Americans from the Civil War to World War II*, by Douglas A. Blackmon, or by watching the documentary *13th*, directed by Ava DuVernay, which is available on Netflix.

■ Join advocacy groups that focus on abolishing mass incarceration. See page 143 for a helpful guide to choosing an organization to support.

■ Contact your state and local representatives to push for repeal of discriminatory laws, including unequal sentencing laws. See page 145 for a helpful guide to contacting your representatives.

■ Volunteer at a nonprofit organization that assists people with reentry after incarceration.

■ Start or join a prison ministry at your church.

Currently, about 2.2 million people are in prisons and jails in the United States. The incarceration rate has been soaring higher since the 1970s.

Source: The Sentencing Project

REFLECTION & JOURNAL SPACE

■ Who do you think of when you hear words like *criminal* or *inmate*?

■ Whose story did you hear (in a film or book or in person as you volunteered) that changed your perspective about incarcerated people?

BLACK LIVES MATTER

You might know . . .

The Black Lives Matter movement gained momentum in August 2014 in Ferguson, Missouri, in response to the police shooting of African American teenager Mike Brown.

But maybe you've never thought about . . .

Black Lives Matter is a movement started by three queer women of color focused on police reform, advocating for human rights for African Americans, and addressing matters of racial justice. These have gained media attention with the advent of cell phone video, but the problem has been ongoing for generations. Black lives are lifted up specifically because of the history of racial discrimination against Black bodies—from slavery to Jim Crow to the current police violence epidemic. All lives won't matter until Black lives matter. The Black Lives Matter movement is also an advocacy movement working toward changes to laws, policies, and practices around issues of race and policing.

"I love my blackness. And yours."

DeRay Mckesson

While more than half of those killed by the police in the US were white, the rate of white people being killed by police was about 2.9 per million people in the population. Compare this with the 6.66 per million rate for Black people and 10.13 per million for Native Peoples.

Source: The Guardian

1 in 65

1 in 65 deaths (or 1.5%) of young Black males is the result of being fatally shot by police.

Source: The Guardian

In a 2015 study, only 65% of the participating police academies provided de-escalation training, while 95% provided firearm training. Police agencies spend roughly 58 hours teaching recruits about firearms and 49 hours teaching defensive tactics. Crisis intervention and de-escalation training are only about 8 hours each.

Source: Police Executive Research Forum

Percent of police academies offering training

De-escalation   Firearms

WHAT YOU CAN DO

■ Find ways to get involved with your local Black Lives Matter (BLM) chapter, or attend a Black Lives Matter rally in your community. Bring your friends and family with you. Listen to the stories being told there.

■ Educate yourself about the BLM movement. Watch the film *Whose Streets?* (directed by Sabaah Folayan, released August 2017). Read the report on the investigation of the Ferguson Police Department by the US Department of Justice.

■ Pay attention to how BLM is talked about in the news, and notice how the movement's work is described differently than that of advocacy groups led by white people.

■ Contact your representatives to advocate for police reform at the local and state levels, especially more funding for de-escalation training. See page 145 for a helpful guide on contacting your representatives.

According to a 2016 report, 1,092 people were killed by the police in the US.

Source: The Guardian

REFLECTION & JOURNAL SPACE

■ Have you been inconvenienced by a Black Lives Matter rally in your community? How does that inconvenience compare with the structural oppression faced by Black people each day?

■ What did you learn from the film *Whose Streets?* or the DOJ's Ferguson report that affected your perspective on the BLM movement?

■ Are you more comfortable asserting "All lives matter" than "Black lives matter"? If so, what might be the root of your discomfort?

CLIMATE CHANGE

You might know . . .

The earth's climate is warming,
and human activity is responsible.

But maybe you've never thought about . . .

The rate of climate change is increasing, outpacing
scientists' predictions. This is happening even as
concern about climate change remains largely
unchanged, even decreasing among people in
certain demographic groups. The scientific reality
is that the climate is warming, and the cause is
human emissions of greenhouse gases. This has
been unchanged for decades. What has changed?
People just don't seem as concerned as they used
to be.

"I dream of a world where the truth is
what shapes people's politics, rather
than politics shaping what people
think is true."

Neil deGrasse Tyson

The average surface temperature of the globe has been steadily increasing since 1975, with the current temperature being 1.69° Fahrenheit above the twentieth-century average.

Source: Climate.gov

Studies of the Arctic have shown decreased land areas covered by snow (down by almost 18% since 1966), higher permafrost temperatures, shrinking glaciers and ice caps, and decreased ice cover of lakes, rivers, and seas. All of these changes have been occurring more rapidly within the past few decades.

Source: Arctic Monitoring and Assessment Program

Globally, the median share of people who say they believe global warming is having a negative impact on people around the world right now is 51%, while only 41% of people in the United States say the same.

51
Global

Percent of people who say they believe global warming is having a negative impact

41
United States

The countries with the greatest carbon dioxide emissions also tend to be where people express the least concern about global warming, with the United States having some of the highest emission rates and one of the lowest concern rates.

Source: Pew Research Center

WHAT YOU CAN DO

- Learn the facts and support them with reliable sources. Don't rely on a web search to do your research for you. Follow reliable scientists and journalists. Go directly to sources that are trustworthy.

- Change your behavior. Drive less. Eat better. Divest from fossil fuel companies. Making personal changes will increase your commitment to climate change activism. Walk the walk.

- Know your representatives' positions and past statements on climate change. Decisions at every level—national, state, and local—have an impact on the outcomes of climate. That also means representatives at every level need to be held accountable.

- Climate science is complicated, and the work of experts is necessary. Donate money to support those experts.

All sixteen years of the twenty-first century rank among the seventeen warmest years on record.

Source: Climate.gov

REFLECTION & JOURNAL SPACE

- What have you done to mitigate your carbon emissions?

- Climate change does not affect everyone in the same ways. What changes have you seen where you live? What do you expect in the future?

- Who do you know that denies climate science? What do you think is the most likely way to engage this person in a discussion about climate?

PATH TO CITIZENSHIP

You might know . . .

Many immigrants are granted
legal citizenship each year.

But maybe you've never thought about . . .

Not everyone can get to this country legally, even if
they follow all the rules, and the path to citizenship
is made even more complex for immigrants whose
temporary legal status has expired. The existing
paths to citizenship for undocumented immigrants
are complicated, burdensome, and costly. It is not
possible to ask undocumented immigrants to "get
back in line" and gain citizenship legally. There is no
clear line to follow, and for some people, no legal path
to citizenship exists under the current system.

"I hereby declare . . . that I will support and defend
the Constitution and laws of the United States
of America . . . that I will bear true faith and
allegiance to the same . . . and that I take this
obligation freely, without any mental reservation
or purpose of evasion; so help me God."

Naturalization Oath of Allegiance
to the United States of America

In 2015, about 730,259 individuals became naturalized citizens of the United States.

Source: US Department of Homeland Security

Many of those naturalized came from India (6%), the Philippines (6%), China (4%), the Dominican Republic (4%), and Vietnam (3%).

Source: US Department of Homeland Security

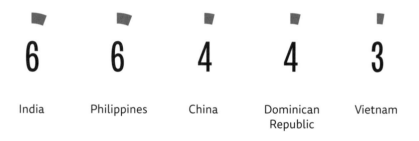

6	6	4	4	3
India	Philippines	China	Dominican Republic	Vietnam

The processing time between submitting an application for citizenship and having a citizenship interview can vary from 5 months to 2 years.

Source: US Immigration

11.3 million

The estimated number of undocumented immigrants in the United States in 2016 was 11.3 million, down from 12.2 million in 2007.

Source: Pew Research Center

WHAT YOU CAN DO

■ Visit the Green Card Voices website at greencardvoices. com, and watch personal video narratives from America's immigrants.

■ Contact your representatives and ask them to sponsor and support immigration reform legislation that offers an expedited path to citizenship for undocumented immigrants. See page 145 for a helpful guide to contacting your representatives.

■ Attend a naturalization ceremony in your city. They are often public events, and the US District Court in your state should have the information posted online.

Of the individuals naturalized in 2015, 15% came from Mexico. This is the highest rate of people naturalized from a single country.

Source: US Department of Homeland Security

REFLECTION & JOURNAL SPACE

■ Whose Green Card Voices story did you hear that affected you, making you see things in a new way?

■ What feels fair or unfair about giving undocumented immigrants an expedited path to citizenship? What personal values do you draw on to define fairness?

■ Do you consider your family's migration story to be "fair"? Why or why not?

SOME HELPFUL DEFINITIONS

The following definitions describe legal terms related to immigration. They are based on information from the US Department of Homeland Security and the American Immigration Council.

■ *Refugee* A person admitted to the United States based upon an inability to return to his or her home country because of a well-founded fear of persecution due to the person's race, membership in a particular social group, political opinion, religion, or national origin.

■ *Asylum seeker* A person already in the United States who is seeking protection based on the same five protected grounds as for refugees. The United States has no limit on the number of individuals who may be granted asylum in a given year, nor are there specific categories for determining who may seek asylum.

■ *Green card holder* Commonly used term for a lawful permanent resident. Green card holders are legally accorded the privilege of residing permanently in the United States. Refugees and asylees are eligible to become lawful permanent residents one year after admission to the United States as a refugee or one year after receiving asylum.

■ *Visa holder* Person with a visa, a document that gives the person permission to stay in the United States for a prescribed amount of time. Some visas are non-immigrant visas; examples include work visas, tourist visas, and student visas. Immigrant visas allow an individual to enter the United States with the potential to apply for a green card and stay as a lawful permanent resident.

■ *DACA* An abbreviation for a "deferred action for childhood arrivals," a federal government policy. Beginning in 2012, the Department of Homeland Security allowed certain people who entered the United States as children to receive deferred action with regard to removal proceedings for a period of time, subject to renewal. The program was rescinded in 2017.

ENVIRONMENTAL REGULATION

You might know ...

Regulations are complicated and burdensome, even if they do help the environment.

But maybe you've never thought about ...

Before the era of the Environmental Protection Agency (EPA) and environmental regulations, toxic chemicals were in widespread public use. (You might remember DDT videos from your childhood.) Indoor and outdoor air was dangerously polluted, and water quality was so bad that a river in Ohio actually caught on fire. Human and environmental health has improved across dozens of metrics, thanks to environmental laws and regulations implemented by federal and state government agencies.

"Why should we tolerate a diet of weak poisons, a home in insipid surroundings, a circle of acquaintances who are not quite our enemies, the noise of motors with just enough relief to prevent insanity? Who would want to live in a world which is just not quite fatal?"

Rachel Carson, *Silent Spring*

1970

Since 1970, the Clean Air Act has been helping to regulate the amount of pollutants released into the air by mobile and stationary sources in order to improve the quality of the United States' air.

The standards set by the act have decreased the number of pollutants in the air, helped make people and the environment healthier, and encouraged development of greener technologies.

Source: US Environmental Protection Agency

1972

The Clean Water Act of 1972 regulates the amount of wastewater expelled by industries and establishes quality standards for all surface waters. This act is mainly meant to keep bodies of water from being polluted by industries.

Source: US Environmental Protection Agency

1974

The Safe Drinking Water Act of 1974 sets standards to which all owners or operators of public water systems must comply in order to protect both aboveground and underground waters that can be or are being used as drinking water.

Source: US Environmental Protection Agency

WHAT YOU CAN DO

■ Learn the regulatory process; it's crucial for influencing environmental law and policy. Comment on docket proceedings, and sign up for newsletters from your state's public utility commission. Learn the agencies in your state and how they operate, and get involved. Few people do the hard work of regulatory activism, so everyone who does it has an impact.

■ Know who provides your electricity, and keep them accountable. Find out what their energy portfolio contains, and demand cleaner sources of energy. If you're part of a co-op, get involved in its meetings.

■ Support local organizations doing regulatory and legal work. Organizations like the Environmental Law and Policy Center spend their time fighting legal and regulatory battles, largely out of the spotlight.

We have a long way to go when it comes to clean air and clean water, but we have accomplished much with these environmental regulations.

REFLECTION & JOURNAL SPACE

■ What environmental threat do you face on a daily basis?
   How can that threat be mitigated?

■ Environmental regulation is often opposed on the grounds
   of the costs it is expected to add to doing business. How
   much is a clean living environment worth?

LIVING WITH A DISABILITY

You might know ...

The Americans with Disabilities Act of 1990 (ADA) was intended to prohibit discrimination and to ensure equal opportunity under the law for persons with disabilities.

But maybe you've never thought about ...

The civil rights of persons with disabilities are still alarmingly contested. Persons living with disabilities are victims of abuse and crime at higher rates and are unemployed at higher rates than the nondisabled. Assumptions built into the architecture of our buildings and the structure of our society prevent persons with disabilities from being able to participate. There is no single social or fiscal program that covers care for persons living with disabilities, so families are often strained by having to create a patchwork of care.

"Every one of us is different in some way, but for those of us who are more different, we have to put more effort into convincing the less different that we can do the same things they can, just differently."

Marlee Matlin

Persons with disabilities suffer violent victimization at 3 times the rate of persons without disabilities. Individuals with cognitive disabilities experience the most violent victimization among persons with disabilities.

Source: US Department of Justice

60% of students with disabilities report experiencing regular bullying, compared with 25% of all students.

Source: The Arc's National Center on Criminal Justice and Disability

Percent of students that report regular bullying

students with disabilities

all students

The rate of unemployment of persons with disabilities has actually increased after the passage of the ADA.

WHAT YOU CAN DO

■ Spend a day or two shadowing a person living with a disability. Make note of unmet accessibility needs. Then advocate for better accessibility in your community.

■ Get involved with the Institute for Human Centered Design and push for the adoption of universal design in your community spaces.

■ Advocate for universal health care and universal basic income, both of which would provide a much-needed safety net for persons with disabilities.

Children with disabilities are 2.9 times more likely to experience sexual violence than their peers.

Source: The Arc's National Center on Criminal Justice and Disability

REFLECTION & JOURNAL SPACE

- ■ Do you think of ability and disability in utilitarian terms, meaning those who produce less are valued less? If so, how can you reframe that thinking to see value in neuro- and physical diversity?

- ■ Are persons with disabilities represented in your workplace? (Remember, not all disability is visible.) If not, what institutional barriers are in place?

THE GEOGRAPHY OF RACE

You might know ...

Americans have the right
to choose where they live.

But maybe you've never thought about ...

The demographic geography of our cities and counties
is not determined by free choice, but rather by racially
discriminatory policies and decisions dating back
decades. Home ownership is one of the main ways
Americans build stability and wealth, but people of
color face barriers and restrictions to home ownership
and wealth building, and therefore can't pass on
generational wealth.

"Two hundred fifty years of slavery. Ninety years
of Jim Crow. Sixty years of separate but equal.
Thirty-five years of racist housing policy. Until
we reckon with our compounding moral debts,
America will never be whole."

Ta-Nehisi Coates

The home ownership gap between white people and people
of color is over 25%. 72% of white households own their
homes, and 46% of households of color own their homes.

Source: Minnesota Homeownership Center

US Homeownership

White
households

Households
of color

Redlining is the practice whereby residents of certain
neighborhoods are denied or receive less financial
services based on the ethnic or racial composition of their
neighborhood, instead of their individual qualities.

Source: The Fair Housing Center of Greater Boston

White flight refers to a national trend in the 1960s and '70s,
when white middle- and upper-class families moved out of
the increasingly diversifying cities and into the suburbs.

Source: The Institute for Research on Poverty

WHAT YOU CAN DO

■ Read *Slavery by Another Name: The Re-enslavement of Black Americans from the Civil War to World War II*, by Douglas A. Blackmon.

■ Research your family's home ownership and wealth-building history. How many generations in your family, if any, have owned homes? How did the first home-owning generation in your family get that home?

■ Look around your neighborhood. Who is represented? Research the history of your neighborhood and the policies that have created the demographics you see today.

■ Contact your representatives to advocate for affordable-housing initiatives in your community. See page 145 for a helpful guide to contacting your representatives.

1920

Racially restrictive covenants were used starting around the 1920s to prevent nonwhite individuals and families from being able to move into dominantly white neighborhoods.

Source: The Fair Housing Center of Greater Boston

REFLECTION & JOURNAL SPACE

■   What did you learn about your neighbors and the demographic history of your neighborhood?

■   Why did you choose to rent or own your home in your
particular neighborhood?

■   Now that you know your family's wealth-building history,
what advantages do you have that you didn't realize before?

ECONOMICS OF EDUCATION

You might know . . .

Inner-city schools are struggling.

But maybe you've never thought about . . .

Most American schools are funded by local property taxes. School districts in high-poverty areas have fewer guidance counselors and psychologists, lower-paid teachers, bigger class sizes, and more run-down facilities than wealthier districts. Students of color are particularly disadvantaged. Coming from a high-poverty district can irreparably damage a child's future, leading to fewer years of education completed, lower lifetime earnings, and higher rates of poverty in adulthood. Those students who are able to attend college are faced with debt loads that can cripple their financial futures.

"All of us in the academy and in the culture as a whole are called to renew our minds if we are to transform educational institutions—and society—so that the way we live, teach, and work can reflect our joy in cultural diversity, our passion for justice, and our love of freedom."

bell hooks

As of 2012, the achievement gaps between white students and students of color were 30% to 40% smaller than in the 1970s. Nonetheless, the gaps are still very large, ranging from 0.5 to 0.9 standard deviations. The largest achievement gap is between white and Black students in twelfth-grade math.

Source: Stanford Center for Education Policy Analysis

The students in the Lexington, Massachusetts, school district perform 3.8 grade levels above the national average. The median family income for this district is $163,000. The racial makeup of the district is 59% white, 33% Asian/other, 4% Latinx, and 4% Black.

3.8 ⬆ Lexington, Massachusetts

2.0 ⬇ Cleveland, Ohio

In contrast, students in the district in Cleveland Municipal, Ohio, perform 2.0 grade levels below average. This district has a $24,000 median family income and the makeup of the community is 67% Black, 16% white, 13% Latinx, and 4% Asian and other.

Source: The New York Times

WHAT YOU CAN DO

■ Find out if your state funds universal pre-K education. Contact your representatives to advocate for more funding for pre-K programs. See page 145 for a helpful guide to contacting your representatives.

■ Volunteer as a tutor or help with an after-school program in your own school district or in a nearby district.

Around 44.2 million Americans are in debt from student loans. The average amount of debt amassed by 2016 college graduates was $37,172 per student.

Source: Student Loan Hero

REFLECTION & JOURNAL SPACE

■ Did you choose the location of your home based on the quality of the school districts there? If such a choice was possible for you, consider the privilege you hold.

■ Do you have student loan debt? If so, what opportunities have you missed because of that debt?

ENVIRONMENTAL JUSTICE

You might know . . .

Pollution of the commons (air, water, soil) negatively affects everyone.

But maybe you've never thought about . . .

Communities of color have significantly increased levels of exposure to polluted air and water. Latinx persons and African Americans are at a higher risk of exposure to air pollutants that are connected to asthma, cardiovascular disease, and lung disease. This is because people of color are twice as likely to live in proximity to hazardous-waste sites and industrial facilities. Children of color are at the highest risk, at rates five to twelve times higher than white children of suffering from lead poisoning and other toxic risks.

"Any harm done to the environment is harm done to humanity."

Pope Francis

Exposure to various air pollutants has been paired with health problems, including cardiovascular disease, negative pregnancy outcomes, and asthma, among other conditions.

Individuals with lower socioeconomic statuses tend to be exposed to higher air pollution concentrations than those with higher socioeconomic statuses.

More than 500,000 children under the age of five have blood lead levels that are above five milliliters per deciliter—the level that triggers a public health response. Remember: no safe blood lead level in children has been identified.

 **5 ml/dl**

Children who are most affected by lead poisoning tend to be from minority populations, come from families with lower income, and live in older houses.

Source: The Center for Disease Control

WHAT YOU CAN DO

■ Reduce your own participation in the pollution of air, water, and soil by conserving energy, avoiding toxic chemicals and products, and reducing consumption (and thereby waste).

■ Recognize, and act, on the *intersectionality* of injustice. Fighting for environmental justice means combating racism and poverty. These problems cannot be solved independently.

■ Support legal efforts—with your money!—under way to combat dumping, pollution reduction, and other institutional means that prop up unfair and inequitable treatment of communities of color.

Latinx populations in the United States are exposed to higher levels of pollutants than other races. Asians and African Americans also experience more exposure to pollutants than white people.

Source: Environmental Health Perspectives

REFLECTION & JOURNAL SPACE

■   What risks do you face based on your local environment?

■   What benefits do you experience based on where you live?

■   How does the fight for racial justice reflect the issue of
      environmental justice?

CAUSES OF DISABILITY

You might know . . .

Millions of Americans
live with disabilities.

But maybe you've never thought about . . .

Persons living with disabilities constitute one of
the largest minorities in the United States. No two
disabilities are the same—each person living with
a disability experiences a unique onset of disability
and a unique way of being in the world. There is also
no universal definition of disability, and disability
is not always visible. Persons with disabilities are
united by the prejudicial way they are perceived and
by the marginalization of their lives. The majority
of persons living with disabilities are not born
with disability, but instead experience life-onset
disability. The key conditions disposing a person
toward disability are poverty, war and conflict, and
environmental disregard.

"From the right to know and the duty
to inquire flows the obligation to act."

Sandra Steingraber, *Living Downstream*

> ■ *Chronically homeless* Individuals with disabilities who either
> experienced continuous homelessness for greater than or
> equal to a year or who experienced upward of four bouts of
> homelessness within the last three years.
>
> Source: US Department of Housing and Urban Development

Only one-third of those chronically homeless found
refuge in shelters. The rest stayed outdoors, in cars,
or in abandoned structures.

Source: US Department of Housing and Urban Development

Approximately 6.7 million individuals with disabilities
worldwide are displaced from their homes due to persecution,
conflict and violence, and human rights violations.

Source: Women's Refugee Commission

WHAT YOU CAN DO

■ When talking about or working with persons with disabilities, always look at the definition of disability being used in that context. For example, the rules for getting a parking permit define disability differently than the rules for getting Medicaid define it.

■ Advocate for workers' rights for migrant farmers—who, along with their children, are vulnerable to the effects of pesticide usage—and other workers at high risk for life-onset disabilities.

■ Reduce your own use of pesticides, toxic household cleaners, and other known contaminants. Advocate for the regulation of environmental contaminants in your city and state.

23

In 2015, 23% of all homeless individuals in the United States were chronically homeless.

Source: US Department of Housing and Urban Development

REFLECTION & JOURNAL SPACE

■ Anyone at any time can become disabled. How does this knowledge change your relationship to disability?

■ Can disability be beautiful?

HEALTH CARE

You might know . . .

Health care costs are rising.

But maybe you've never thought about . . .

Millions of Americans live without health insurance—just one medical emergency away from financial disaster. Our current system ensures that only those with the most privilege will receive the best care. Food deserts—areas where people have limited access to a variety of healthful and affordable food—are most often found in the poorest parts of our communities, and they contribute to health disparity. Women and children are particularly disadvantaged, and the infant mortality rate in the U.S. is alarmingly high. Health risks for women are exacerbated when women are denied access to safe and affordable reproductive health care and when women's rights are curtailed.

"The United States is the only major country on Earth not to guarantee healthcare to all people as a right. . . . We've got to go further . . . and say that if you are an American, you are guaranteed healthcare as a right, not a privilege."

Sen. Bernie Sanders

13

13% of adults aged 18–64, or 25.1 million people,
are uninsured (as of 2015).

Source: Prison Policy Initiative

An ER visit will cost the uninsured person greater
than $800, and 60% of visits cost greater than $1,550.

Source: Public Library of Science

34

Per capita lifetime health care costs for women are
34% higher than for men.

Source: Health Services Research

The USDA's Food Access Research Atlas and Food
Environment Atlas will show you statistics on food
environment around the country, including the
location of food deserts in your city.

The infant mortality rate in the United States is
approximately 5.8 deaths per 1,000 live births,
which is higher than other developed countries,
for example, Iceland: 2.1; Singapore: 2.4; South
Korea: 3.0; Germany: 3.4, Denmark: 4.0; Canada: 4.6.

Source: Central Intelligence Agency

WHAT YOU CAN DO

- Contact your congressional representatives and senators, and ask them to sponsor and support legislation for universal, affordable health coverage for all Americans. See page 145 for a helpful guide to contacting your representatives.

- Donate money and volunteer your time at the free clinics in your community.

- Donate fresh produce, not just nonperishable and packaged goods, to your local food pantry. Do it often.

63% of Americans don't have enough savings to cover a $500 emergency.

Source: Forbes

REFLECTION & JOURNAL SPACE

- When was your family's last health emergency? What sort of care did you receive? How did you cover the costs?

- In what way is your health, and your access to health care, a privilege? Are you able-bodied? Can you afford a doctor's visit if you get sick or injured? Do you have access to fresh, healthful food you can afford?

- Is health care a human right? What are the consequences of saying it is? What are the consequences of saying it isn't?

GUIDE

CHOOSING AN ORGANIZATION TO SUPPORT OR JOIN

Here are some questions to ask when looking for the right organization to support or join.

- Who is in leadership (staff and board)? Do they represent the group they're advocating for? Who is the CEO, and how is that person connected?

- Follow the money. Who are the funding sources (individuals, corporations, other groups)? Of the money donated to the group, how much goes to the cause they're advocating for?

- What is the group's history of involvement with the community? Have they been in the community for a long time, or are they brand new? If they are brand new, why? Have their focus and core commitments changed over time? If so, why?

- Is the organization well known within the community they purport to serve? How much are they invested in it?

- Show up and observe. Who is most present? What is the first action asked of you?

- Pay attention to how they recruit and vet volunteers.

- Whose voices are amplified by this group? Who is silenced by the work this group does?

- What information resources are being put out by this organization? Have they been fact-checked?

■ Who is the organization in coalitions with? Who are their partners?

■ What does the group's social-media footprint look like? What do they share, and who engages with that material? How has the organization shown up in the news?

Also, as you evaluate organizations, remember that no movement has universal agreement about which organizations are the best.

GUIDE
CONTACTING YOUR REPRESENTATIVES

Find out who represents you at the local, state, and federal level.

- Visit senate.gov and house.gov to search for your federal congress persons and senators. Your state legislature will have a similar web tool for finding your state representatives.

- You are free to contact any member of congress, but you will be most effective when you contact legislators who represent you directly. Be sure to state your full name and zip code when you call, or include it in your letter or email, to make it clear that you live in the relevant district.

- Once you learn them, save your legislators' phone numbers in your cell phone, to make the process even quicker and form a more regular habit.

- Before you call, write out word-for-word what you want to say, and keep it to a few sentences. This will help with nerves, and ensure that your message is clear.

- Be kind and courteous to whoever answers the phone.

- When writing a letter or email, be sure to use your own words. There are helpful templates and scripts online, but a personal touch will increase the impact of your letter. Details about how the bill or issue affects you personally are particularly effective.

- Don't forget social media. By commenting on your representative's Facebook page, or replying to a tweet, you make your questions and concerns visible to other constituents and help spark conversation.

GUIDE
SHOWING UP FOR THE FIRST TIME IN AN ACTIVIST SPACE

- Follow and observe. You are there to watch, listen, and learn, unless asked or prompted otherwise by the leaders. Remember that the stakes are likely different for you than for others.

- Be prepared to be uncomfortable. Ask yourself why you're feeling uncomfortable. Use the experience to explore further self-examination and education.

- If you find yourself overwhelmed, emotional, or triggered, you have permission to leave. Step back and care for yourself, and come back again when you are ready.

- Do your research. Don't expect the people already doing the work to educate you.

- Pay attention to who the leaders are. Whose voice is amplified? Whose voice is silenced?

- Don't make yourself a spokesperson for the movement. Instead amplify the voices of those already leading.

- Pay attention to who else is there.

- Ask questions.

- Respond to specific calls to action or requests rather than deciding on your own what is needed.

- Use good judgment and common sense.

GUIDE
PARTICIPATING IN YOUR FIRST PROTEST

- Remember: the point of a protest is to be disruptive. Nonviolent does not mean non-disruptive or non-confrontational. An acceptable protest is an oxy-moron.

- Identify the Marshals, and other leaders, so that you know who to follow and/or contact in case of concern.

- Use good judgment:
  - Be cautious of people soliciting funds
  - Don't leave with people that you don't know
  - Bring a buddy

- Dress comfortably: wear good shoes and weather-appropriate clothing.

- Be on the lookout for people who are there for nefarious reasons.

- Plan how you'll get safely to and from, and where you'll meet your group if you get separated.

- Do research in advance about the background on the issue, and the plans for the protest.

- Don't talk to the press or the police, unless given specific instructions by the organizers.

- Decide ahead of time whether you're willing to risk arrest.

- Respect and honor the feelings and expressions of those for whom the stakes are the most high.

- Don't engage with counter-protesters.

- Know your rights. The ACLU offers a helpful pocket guide for protestors called *Know Your Rights: Demonstrations and Protests*. It's available at https://www.aclu.org/sites/default/files/field_pdf_file/kyr_protests.pdf.

- You have permission to leave if you are overwhelmed or afraid, or if the event changes in a way that makes you uncomfortable.

REFERENCES

WE'RE ALL IMMIGRANTS

"QuickFacts: United States." United States Census Bureau. Accessed June 20, 2017. https://www.census.gov/quickfacts/table/RHI325215/00.

Gates, Henry Louis Jr. "Slavery, by the Numbers." The Root. Feburary 20, 2014. Accessed June 16, 2017. http://www.theroot.com/slavery-by-the-numbers-1790874492.

ARE WE POST-RACIAL?

"Calendar of Ethnic Holidays." Wake Forest University. 2017. Accessed June 20, 2017. http://college.wfu.edu/aes/calendar-of-ethnic-holidays/.

"Poverty Rate by Race/Ethnicity." Kaiser Family Foundation. 2017. Accessed June 2, 2017. http://www.kff.org/other/state-indicator/poverty-rate-by-raceethnicity/.

"Unemployment rate and employment-population ration vary by race and ethnicity." Bureau of Labor Statistics. 2017. Accessed June 16, 2017. https://www.bls.gov/opub/ted/2017/unemployment-rate-and-employment-population-ratio-vary-by-race-and-ethnicity.htm.

Wagner, Peter, and Bernadette Rabuy. "Mass Incarceration: The Whole Pie 2017." Prison Policy Initiative. March 14, 2017. Accessed June 2, 2017. https://www.prisonpolicy.org/reports/pie2017.html.

NATIVE LAND

"Indian Lands of the United States." U.S. Department of the Interior. Last Modified February 7, 2017. Accessed June 14, 2017. https://nationalmap.gov/small_scale/mld/indlanp.html.

"Oak Flat/Apache Leap." Earthworks. Accessed June 15, 2017. https://www.earthworksaction.org/voices/detail/oak_flat_apache_leap#.WUBxXGjyvIU.

McAuliff, Michael. "Defense Bill Passes, Giving Sacred Native American Sites to Mining Company." Huffington Post. December 12, 2014. Accessed June 15, 2017." http://www.huffingtonpost.com/2014/12/12/defense-bill-passes-rio-tinto_n_6317946.html.

WATER

"Lead Poisoning and Health." World Health Organization. Last Modified September 2016. Accessed June 20, 2017. http://www.who.int/mediacentre/factsheets/fs379/en/.

Cousins, Farron. "America is Suffering From a Very Real Water Crisis That Few are Acknowledging." Desmog. January 24, 2017. Accessed June 20, 2017. https://www.desmogblog.com/2017/01/24/america-suffering-very-real-water-crisis-few-are-acknowledging.

McGraw, George. "For These Americans, Clean Water is a Luxury." The New York Times. October 20, 2016. Accessed June 20, 2017.https://www.nytimes.com/2016/10/20/opinion/for-these-americans-clean-water-is-a-luxury.html.

LGBTQIA EQUALITY

"Why the Equality Act?" Human Rights Campaign. 2017. Accessed May 29, 2017. http://www.hrc.org/resources/why-the-equality-act.

"Joint Adoption Laws." Equality Council. 2017. Accessed May 29, 2017. http://www.familyequality.org/get_informed/resources/equality_maps/joint_adoption_laws/.

"Addressing Stigma: A Blueprint for Improving HIV/STD Prevention and Care Outcomes for Black & Latino Gay Men." National Alliance of State and Territorial AIDS Directors. May 2014. Accessed May 29, 2017. https://www.nastad.org/sites/default/files/NASTAD-NCSD-Report-Addressing-Stigma-May-2014.pdf.

"LGBTQIA Resource Center Glossary." The Lesbian, Gay, Bisexual, Transgender, Queer, Intersex, Asexual Resource Center at the University of California, Davis. August 8, 2016. Accessed May 29, 2017. http://lgbtqia.ucdavis.edu/educated/glossary.html.

ABLEISM

Davis, Lennard J., *Enforcing Normalcy: Disability, Deafness, and the Body* (New York: Verso, 1995).

"What is Ableism? Five Things About Ableism You Should Know." FWD/Forward.November 19, 2010. Accessed June 16, 2017. http://disabledfeminists.com/2010/11/19/what-is-ableism-five-things-about-ableism-you-should-know/.

"Screening tests (Checking Your Baby's Health Before Birth)." Women and Children's Health Network, Last Modified November 3, 2016. Accessed June 23, 2017. http://www.cyh.com/HealthTopics/HealthTopicDetails.aspx?p=438&np=459&id=2760#what.

WHITE SUPREMACY

Kochhar, Rakesh, and Richard Fry. "Wealth Inequality has Widened Along Racial, Ethnic Lines Since End of Great Recession." Pew Research Center. December 12, 2014. Accessed June 9, 2017. http://www.pewresearch.org/fact-tank/2014/12/12/racial-wealth-gaps-great-recession/.

"Median Household Income in the United States in 2015, by Race or Ethnic Group (in U.S. Dollars)." The Statistics Portal. 2017. Accessed June 3, 2017. https://www.statista.com/statistics/233324/median-household-income-in-the-united-states-by-race-or-ethnic-group/.

LIFE FOR NATIVE PEOPLES

Krogstad, Jens Manuel. "One-in-Four Native Americans and Alaska Natives are Living in Poverty." Pew Research Center. June 13, 2014. Accessed June 12, 2017. http://www.pewresearch.org/fact-tank/2014/06/13/1-in-4-native-americans-and-alaska-natives-are-living-in-poverty/.

"Public High School Graduation Rates." National Center for Education Statistics. Last Modified April 2017. Accessed June 13, 2017. https://nces.ed.gov/programs/coe/indicator_coi.asp.

Cowlitz Indian Tribe. "Native American Community." Washington Coalition of Sexual Assault Programs. Last Modified April 26, 2016. Accessed June 12, 2017. http://www.wcsap.org/native-american-community.

SEXUAL VIOLENCE

National Sexual Violence Resource Center. "What Is Sexual Violence?" 2016. Accessed June 26, 2017. http://www.nsvrc.org/sites/default/files/saam_2016_what-is-sexual-violence_0.pdf.

RAINN "Victims of Sexual Violence: Statistics" 2016. Accessed June 26, 2017. https://www.rainn.org/statistics/victims-sexual-violence.

"The Facts." Polaris. 2017. Accessed July 10, 2017. https://polarisproject.org/facts.

TRANSGENDER EQUALITY

Kralik, Joellen. "'Bathroom Bill' Legislative Tracking: 2017 State Legislation." The National Conference of State Legislatures. April 12, 2017. Accessed June 9, 2017. http://www.ncsl.org/research/education/-bathroom-bill-legislative-tracking635951130.aspx.

Bolles, Alexandra. "Violence Against Transgender People and People of Color is Disproportionately High, LGBTQH Murder Rate Peaks." Gay and Lesbian Alliance Against Defamation. June 4, 2012. Accessed June 9, 2017. https://www.glaad.org/blog/violence-against-transgender-people-and-people-color-disproportionately-high-lgbtqh-murder-rate.

Haas, Ann P., Philip L. Rodgers, and Jody L. Herman. "Suicide Attempts Among Transgender and Gender Non-Conforming Adults: Findings of the National Transgender Discrimination Survey." The Williams Institute. January 2014. Accessed June 6, 2017. http://williamsinstitute.law.ucla.edu/wp-content/uploads/AFSP-Williams-Suicide-Report-Final.pdf.

"LGBTQIA Resource Center Glossary." The Lesbian, Gay, Bisexual, Transgender, Queer, Intersex, Asexual Resource Center at the University of California, Davis. August 8, 2016. Accessed May 29, 2017. http://lgbtqia.ucdavis.edu/educated/glossary.html.

THE GENDER WAGE GAP

U.S. Census Bureau, 2015 American Community Survey 1-Year Estimates and U.S. Census Bureau, Current Population Survey, Annual Social and Economic Supplements, Table P-38.

EQUALITY AND EQUITY

Daniels, Jessie. "White Women and Arrifmative Action: Prime Beneficiaries and Opponents" RacismReview. 2014. Accessed June 26, 2017. http://www.racismreview.com/blog/2014/03/11/white-women-affirmative-action/.

Ajinkya, Julie. "Unequal Pay Day for Black and Latina Women" Center for American Progress. 2012. Accessed June 16, 2017. https://www.americanprogress.org/issues/women/news/2012/04/16/11437/unequal-pay-day-for-black-and-latina-women/.

"Voter Suppression Laws: What's New Since the 2012 Presidential Election" American Civil Liberties Union. 2017. Accessed June 26, 2017. https://www.aclu.org/map/voter-suppression-laws-whats-new-2012-presidential-election.

NATIVE PEOPLES' RIGHTS

World Heritage Encyclopedia. "List of Unrecognized Tribes in the United States" Accessed June 26, 2017. http://www.worldlibrary.org/articles/list_of_unrecognized_tribes_in_the_united_states.

Native News Online Staff. "Tribal Equal Access to Voting Act of 2015." NativeNewsOnline.net. May 21, 2015. Accessed June 20, 2017. http://nativenewsonline.net/currents/tribal-equal-access-to-voting-act-of-2015/.

WOMEN IN GOVERNMENT

Center for American Women and Politics. "Women in Elective Office 2017." Accessed June 16, 2017. http://cawp.rutgers.edu/women-elective-office-2017.

"Women in International Parliaments." Inter-Parliamentary Union. June 1, 2017. Accessed June 9, 2017. http://www.ipu.org/wmn-e/classif.htm.

CONTRIBUTIONS OF IMMIGRANTS

Archives of Rudolph W. Giuliani, nyc.gov.

Fairchild, Caroline. "16 Iconic American Companies Founded by Immigrants." The Huffington Post. April 15, 2013. Accessed June 15, 2017. http://www.huffingtonpost.com/2013/04/22/american-companies-founded-by-immigrants_n_3116172.html.

"Open for Business: How Immigrants are Driving Small Business Creation in the United States." The Partnership for a New American Economy. August 2012. http://www.newamericaneconomy.org/wp-content/uploads/2013/07/openforbusiness.pdf.

Costa, Daniel, David Cooper, and Heidi Shierholz. "Facts About Immigration and the U.S. Economy: Answers to Frequently Asked Questions." Economic Policy Institute. August 12, 2017. Accessed May 23, 2017. http://www.epi.org/publication/immigration-facts/.

BULLYING OF LGBTQIA YOUTH

"LGBT Bullying Statistics." NoBullying.com. Last Modified November 7, 2016. Accessed June 15, 2017. https://nobullying.com/lgbt-bullying-statistics/.

Cook, Currey. "Fighting Homelessness Among LGBTQ Youth." Lambda Legal. December 1, 2014. Accessed June 4, 2017. http://www.lambdalegal.org/blog/20141201_fighting-homelessness-among-lgbtq-youth.

MENTAL HEALTH

"Module 2: A Brief History of Mental Illness and the U.S. Mental Health Care System." Unite for Sight. 2015. Accessed May 16, 2017. http://www.uniteforsight.org/mental-health/module2#_ftnref1.

"Mental Health and the Role of the States" The Pew Charitable Trusts and the John D. and Catherine T. MacArthur Foundation. June 2015. Accessed May 16, 2017. http://www.pewtrusts.org/~/media/assets/2015/06/mentalhealthandroleofstatesreport.pdf.

Hedden, Sarra L., et al. "Behavioral Health Trends in the United States: Results from the 2014 National Survey on Drug Use and Health. Substance Abuse and mental Health Services Administration. 2015. Accessed June 15, 2017. https://www.samhsa.gov/data/sites/default/files/NSDUH-FRR1-2014/NSDUH-FRR1-2014.pdf.

Skowyra, R. Kathleen, and Joseph J. Cocozza. "Blueprint for Change: A Comprehensive Model for the Identification and Treatment of Youth with Mental Health Needs in Contact with the Juvenile Justice System." The National Center for Mental Health and Juvenile Justice. 2007. Accessed June 15, 2017. https://www.ncmhjj.com/wp-content/uploads/2013/07/2007_Blueprint-for-Change-Full-Report.pdf.

WOMEN IN POVERTY

"Nonelderly Adult Poverty Rates." Henry J. Kaiser Family Foundation. 2015. Accessed June 23, 2017. http://www.kff.org/other/state-indicator/adult-poverty-rate-by-gender/?currentTimeframe=0&sortModel=%7B%22colId%22:%22Location%22,%22sort%22:%22asc%22%7D.

Tucker, Jasmine, and Caitlin Lowell. "National Snapshot: Poverty Among Women & Families, 2015." National Women's Law Center. September 14, 2016. Accessed June 23, 2017. https://nwlc.org/resources/national-snapshot-poverty-among-women-families-2015/.

Reilly, Katie. "Sesame Street Reaches Out to 2.7 Million American Children With an Incarcerated Parent." Pew Research Center. June 21, 2013. Accessed June 5, 2017. http://www.pewresearch.org/fact-tank/2013/06/21/sesame-street-reaches-out-to-2-7-million-american-children-with-an-incarcerated-parent/.

PRISON INDUSTRIAL COMPLEX

Wagner, Peter, and Bernadette Rabuy. "Following the Money of Mass Incarceration." Prison Policy Initiative. January 25, 2017. Accessed June 5, 2017. https://www.prisonpolicy.org/reports/money.html.

"Criminal: How Lockup Quotas and 'Low-Crime Taxes' Guarantee Profits for Private Prison Corporations." In the Public Interest. September 19, 2013. Accessed June 14, 2017. https://www.inthepublicinterest.org/criminal-how-lockup-quotas-and-low-crime-taxes-guarantee-profits-for-private-prison-corporations/.

Davis, Lois M., et al. "Evaluating the Effectiveness of Correctional Education: A Meta-Analysis of Programs That Provide Education to Incarcerated Adults." RAND Corporation. 2013. Accessed June 14, 2017. http://www.rand.org/pubs/research_reports/RR266.html.

WAR ON DRUGS

Wagner, Peter, and Bernadette Rabuy. "Mass Incarceration: The Whole Pie 2017." Prison Policy Initiative. March 14, 2017. Accessed June 12, 2017. https://www.prisonpolicy.org/reports/pie2017.html.

"Criminal Justice Fact Sheet." National Association for the Advancement of Colored People. 2017. Accessed June 22, 2017. http://www.naacp.org/criminal-justice-fact-sheet/.

RACE AND INCARCERATION

"Criminal Justice Facts." The Sentencing Project. 2017. Accessed June 12, 2017. http://www.sentencingproject.org/criminal-justice-facts/.

Wagner, Peter, and Alison Walsh. "States of Incarceration: The Global Context 2016." Prison Policy Initiative. June 16, 2016. Accessed June 23, 2017. https://www.prisonpolicy.org/global/2016.html.

Mauer, Marc, and Ryan S. King. "Uneven Justice: State Rates of Incarceration by Race and Ethnicity." The Sentencing Project. July 2007. Accessed June 15, 2017. http://www.sentencingproject.org/wp-content/uploads/2016/01/Uneven-Justice-State-Rates-of-Incarceration-by-Race-and-Ethnicity.pdf.

BLACK LIVES MATTER

"The Counted: People Killed by Police in the US." The Guardian. 2016. Accessed May 30, 2017. https://www.theguardian.com/us-news/ng-interactive/2015/jun/01/the-counted-police-killings-us-database.

Swaine, Jon, Oliver Laughland, Jamiles Lartey, and Ciara McCarthy. "Young Black Men Killed by US Police at Highest Rate in Year of 1,134 Deaths." The Guardian. December 31, 2015. Accessed May 31, 2017. https://www.theguardian.com/us-news/2015/dec/31/the-counted-police-killings-2015-young-black-men.

"Re-Engineering Training On Police Use of Force." Police Executive Research Forum. August 2015. Accessed June 1, 2017. http://www.policeforum.org/assets/reengineeringtraining1.pdf.

CLIMATE CHANGE

Dahlman, LuAnn. "Climate Change: Global Temperature. Climate.gov. April 19, 2017. Accessed June 22, 2017. https://www.climate.gov/news-features/understanding-climate/climate-change-global-temperature.

"Arctic Climate Issues 2011: Changes in Arctic Snow, Water, Ice and Permafrost." Arctic Monitoring and Assessment Program. 2012. Accessed June 22, 2017. http://www.amap.no/documents/doc/arctic-climate-issues-2011-changes-in-arctic-snow-water-ice-and-permafrost/129.

Wike, Richard. "What the World Thinks About Climate Change in 7 Charts." Pew Research Center. April 18, 2016. Accessed June 22, 2017. http://www.pewresearch.org/fact-tank/2016/04/18/what-the-world-thinks-about-climate-change-in-7-charts/.

PATH TO CITIZENSHIP

"Table 20. Petitions for Naturalized Filed, Persons Naturalized, and Petitions for N Naturalization Denied: Fiscal Years 1907 to 2015." U.S. Department of Homeland Security. December 15, 2016. Accessed May 17, 2017. https://www.dhs.gov/immigration-statistics/yearbook/2015/table20.

"Table 21. Persons Naturalized by Region and Country of Birth: Fiscal Years 2013 to 2015." U.S. Department of Homeland Security. December 15, 2016. Accessed May 17, 2017. https://www.dhs.gov/immigration-statistics/yearbook/2015/table21.

"U.S. Citizenship & Naturalization Process." U.S. Immigration. 2017. Accessed May 17, 2017. https://www.immigrationdirect.com/immigrationresources/U-S-citizenship-naturalization-process.jsp.

Krogstad, Jens Manuel, Jeffrey S. Passel, and D'vera Cohn. "5 Facts About Illegal Immigration in the U.S." Pew Research Center. April 27, 2017. Accessed June 1, 2017. http://www.pewresearch.org/fact-tank/2017/04/27/5-facts-about-illegal-immigration-in-the-u-s/.

"Definition of Terms." U.S. Department of Homeland Security. Last updated November, 3, 2016. Accessed July 7, 2017. https://www.dhs.gov/immigration-statistics/data-standards-and-definitions/definition-terms#.

"How the United States Immigration System Works." American Immigration Council. August 12, 2016. Accessed July 7, 2017. https://www.americanimmigrationcouncil.org/research/how-united-states-immigration-system-works.

ENVIRONMENTAL REGULATION

"Clean Air Act Overview: Progress Cleaning the Air." United States Environmental Protection Agency. Last Modified February 16, 2017. Accessed June 20, 2017. https://www.epa.gov/clean-air-act-overview/progress-cleaning-air-and-improving-peoples-health.

"Laws & Regulations: Summary of the Clean Water Act." United States Environmental Protection Agency. Last Modified February 7, 2017. Accessed June 20, 2017. https://www.epa.gov/laws-regulations/summary-clean-water-act.

Laws & Regulations: Summary of the Safe Drinking Water Act." United States Environmental Protection Agency. Last Modified February 7, 2017. Accessed June 20, 2017. https://www.epa.gov/laws-regulations/summary-safe-drinking-water-act.

LIVING WITH A DISABILITY

"Disability Statistics." United States Department of Labor Office of Disability Employment Policy. 2017. Accessed June 23, 2017. https://www.dol.gov/odep/.

Harrell, Erika. "Crime Against Persons with Disabilities, 2009 – 2012 – Statistical Tables." U.S. Department of Justice. February 2014. Accessed June 10, 2017. https://www.bjs.gov/content/pub/pdf/capd0912st.pdf.

"Violence, Abuse and Bullying Affecting People with Intellectual/ Developmental Disabilities: A Call to Action for the Criminal Justice Community." The Arc's National Center on Criminal Justice and Disability. 2015. Accessed June 23, 2017. http://www.thearc.org/document. doc?id=5145.

GEOGRAPHY OF RACE

Skobba, Kim. "Understanding Homeownership Disparities Among Racial and Ethnic Groups." Minnesota Homeownership Center. 2013. Accessed May 30, 2017. http://www.hocmn.org/wp-content/uploads/2013/11/ REPORT_UnderstandingHomeownershipDisparities.pdf.

"1934 – 1968: FHA Mortgage Insurance Requirements Utilize Redlining." The Fair Housing Center of Greater Boston. Accessed May 31, 2017. http:// www.bostonfairhousing.org/timeline/1934-1968-FHA-Redlining.html.

"1920s – 1948: Racially Restrictive Covenants." The Fair Housing Center of Greater Boston. Accessed May 31, 2017. http://www.bostonfairhousing.org/ timeline/1920s1948-Restrictive-Covenants.html.

Blakeslee, Jan. "'White Flight' to the Suburbs: A Demographic Approach." Institute for Research on Poverty Newsletter. 1979. Accessed May 31, 2017. http://www.irp.wisc.edu/publications/focus/pdfs/foc32a.pdf.

ECONOMICS OF EDUCATION

"The Educational Opportunity Monitoring Project: Racial and Ethnic Achievement Gaps." Stanford Center for Education Policy Analysis. 2013. Accessed June 9, 2017. http://cepa.stanford.edu/educational-opportunity-monitoring-project/achievement-gaps/race/#first.

Rich, Motoko, Amanda Cox, and Matthew Bloch. "Money, Race and Success: How Your School District Compares." The New York Times. April 29, 2016. Accessed June 9, 2017. https://www.nytimes.com/interactive/2016/04/29/upshot/money-race-and-success-how-your-school-district-compares.html.

"A Look at the Shocking Student Loan Debt Statistics for 2017." Student Loan Hero. 2017. Accessed May 30, 2017. https://studentloanhero.com/student-loan-debt-statistics/.

ENVIRONMENTAL JUSTICE

Hajat, Anjum et al. "Air Pollution and Individual and Neighborhood Socioeconomic Status: Evidence from the Multi-Ethnic Study of Atherosclerosis (MESA)." Environmental Health Perspectives 121, no. 11-12 (2013): 1325-1333. Accessed June 20, 2017. https://ehp.niehs.nih.gov/wp-content/uploads/121/11-12/ehp.1206337.pdf.

Bell, Michelle L., and Keita Ebisu. "Environmental Inequality in Exposures to Airborne Particulate Matter Components in the United States." Environmental Health Perspectives 120, no. 12 (2012): 1699-1704. Accessed June 20,2017. https://ehp.niehs.nih.gov/wp-content/uploads/120/12/ehp.1205201.pdf.

"Lead." Centers for Disease Control and Prevention. Last Modified February 9, 2017. Accessed June 20, 2017. https://www.cdc.gov/nceh/lead/.

"Blood Lead Levels – United States, 1999–2002." Centers for Disease Control. Last Modified May 26, 2005. Accessed June 20, 2017. https://www.cdc.gov/mmwr/preview/mmwrhtml/mm5420a5.htm.

CAUSES OF DISABILITY

"The 2015 Annual Homeless Assessment Report (AHAR) to Congress." The U.S. Department of Housing and Urban Development. November 2015. Accessed June 22, 2017. https://www.hudexchange.info/resources/documents/2015-AHAR-Part-1.pdf.

Refugees with Disabilities." Women's Refugee Commission. Last Modified February 19, 2016. Accessed June 20, 2017. https://www.womensrefugeecommission.org/disabilities/disabilities-fact-sheet.

HEALTH CARE

Ward B. W., T. C. Clarke, C. N. Nugent, and J. S. Schiller. "Early release of selected estimates based on data from the 2015 National Health Interview Survey." National Center for Health Statistics. May 2016. Accessed June 16, 2017. http://www.cdc.gov/nchs/nhis.htm.

Caldwell N., T. Srebotnjak, T. Wang, R. Hsia. "'How Much Will I Get Charged for This?' Patient Charges for Top Ten Diagnoses in the Emergency Department." PLOS ONE. 2013. Accessed July 16, 2017. https://doi.org/10.1371/journal.pone.0055491.

McGrath, Maggie. "63% Of Americans Don't Have Enough Savings To Cover A $500 Emergency." Forbes. 2016. Accessed June 16, 2017. https://www.forbes.com/sites/maggiemcgrath/2016/01/06/63-of-americans-dont-have-enough-savings-to-cover-a-500-emergency/#2f329e94e0d9.

"Country Comparison: Infant Mortality Rate." Central Intelligence Agency. 2016. Accessed May 16, 2017. https://www.cia.gov/library/publications/the-world-factbook/rankorder/2091rank.html.